Further Traditions of
Trinity and Leith

Leith also has its West End in Trinity
and Laverockbank, and several neat little
residential areas here and there, with
elegant villas, dignified porches and
windows overlooking well-kept gardens.

Albert Mackie, quoted in *Faces
of Leith*, text by Sheila Mackay, 1986

At Canonmills we spy ye plain
But sune ye're lost to sicht again
Until we see

Doun by Leith Docks the swans that glide
To mark your meetin' wi' the tide,
Your journey's end.

From 'To the Water o' Leith',
in *Rhymes o' Auld Reekie* by
Douglas Fraser

This second volume is also dedicated
to my mother who died, in her
95th year, in 1987 and whose memories of her childhood years at
Miss Yule's School in Trinity have
been incorporated in the text.

Further Traditions of Trinity and Leith

JOYCE M. WALLACE

JOHN DONALD PUBLISHERS LTD.
EDINBURGH

ISBN 0 85976 282 3

British Library Cataloguing in Publication Data
Wallace, Joyce M. (Joyce Moyra) *1925-*
Further traditions of Trinity and Leith.
1. Edinburgh. Leith, to 1984
I. Title
941.34

Typeset by Print Origination (NW) Ltd., Formby, Liverpool
Printed in Great Britain by Bell & Bain Ltd., Glasgow

Contents

Acknowledgements

MY thanks go to the following for all their help in the preparation of this book: the staff of the Edinburgh Room, Edinburgh Central Public Library; the Assistant Librarian, the Royal Scottish Academy; Arnot Wilson, Edinburgh City Archivist; Roland A. Paxton, Department of Highways, Lothian Regional Council; A.J. Downie, Water & Drainage Department, Lothian Regional Council; I.J. Douglas, Secretary, Waddies of Edinburgh; F.L.M. Reynolds, Headmaster, Cargilfield School; Mrs Enid Wilson, granddaughter of the Rev. Daniel Charles Darnell; Captain A.S. Hamilton, Master, Trinity House of Leith; and Miss Elaine Finnie, Assistant Keeper of Social History, Huntly House Museum, Edinburgh.

Except where otherwise stated, photographs are by the author.

Front cover illustrations (left to right): South Leith Church, Pilrig House, Starbank Park and House, Leith Fort.
Back cover: The Old Chain Pier Sign.

Introduction

IT is five years since the publication of *Traditions of Trinity and Leith*. In that time changes have taken place in Leith (where they have been mainly for the better) and also, on a much smaller scale, in Trinity, a beautiful and historic district with its own highly individual character, which has been consistently neglected by the historians of Edinburgh.

As far as Leith is concerned, much has been done imaginatively to fill the ubiquitous gap sites which for far too long had given the port an uncared-for and derelict appearance. Disused industrial buildings such as stores and warehouses, still in total harmony with their environment, have been upgraded into attractive living apartments for a population which, after a serious decline, is now once more healthily increasing, and new business and workshop units have been created in former schools, factories and other redundant structures, thus offering opportunities for investment and employment in a hitherto depressed and dispirited area of the city.

An enlightened emphasis is now being placed on conservation and adaptation rather than on demolition, and this change in attitude has been translated into practical improvements on the ground by the work of the happily conceived Leith Project (operating with the assistance of the Scottish Development Agency) which marked the completion of its five-year regeneration plan for Leith in 1986 by merging with the Leith Enterprise Trust. There is still a great deal to be done but progress so far, including that carried out by private developers, is such that Leith and its people can look to the future with confidence and a degree of optimism which less than ten years ago would not have been foreseen.

In Trinity the picture is rather different. There has

been some loss (e.g. Denham Green House) and some ill-advised new building (e.g. the site of Denham Green House where the sardine tin syndrome has been taken as a model). But by far the greatest threat to the whole district and its environs was the proposed infilling of Wardie Bay (immediately in front of Trinity) to reclaim an area of land as large as five hundred acres from the navigable (and wind-swept) waters of the Firth of Forth on which it was intended to impose houses, offices, hotel-conference-and-exhibition centres, shops, roads and facilities for recreation and entertainment. This was later, as a result of public protest, modified to 130 acres with an 80-acre lagoon between it and the waterfront. The Wardie Bay reclamation plans which, if implemented, would have turned Trinity into a disaster area and destroyed its unique character beyond recall, were rejected in March 1990 by Lothian Regional Council. Permission was, however, granted for development on ground at the Victoria Dock in Leith and for a marina village and an industrial unit complex immediately to the west of Trinity at Granton where a decision to make appropriate use of a run-down area is to be welcomed.

A major restructuring project in Leith is the development of the former Central Station site at the foot of Leith Walk to create large-scale leisure and shopping facilities "under one roof" for the locality itself and with the aim of attracting to it visitors from a much wider area. And as the corner clocktower and part of the original facade (as well as the listed buildings in Duke Street) are fortunately being retained, this famous landmark will remain – a substantial memorial to its long-lost days as a crowded branch line railway terminus. Passenger trains were withdrawn in 1952 and its final role as a maintenance yard lasted for only twenty years thereafter.

Such are the current trends and changes, by no means without signs of hope, in Leith and Trinity, but history continues to reassert itself as the sound foundation on which to base the future, both in building developments and in the way of life of its people who have chosen to make their homes within sight or hailing distance of the sea. So it is hoped that a second volume, which in some ways has almost 'written itself', will be deemed not unacceptable—if only to expand the scope, repair the omissions and amend the errors of the first! Buildings and persons already mentioned are here referred to only in the context of additional material concerning them and the history of such habitations as Trinity Grove and Pilrig House is therefore not repeated. A reading list has been included.

J. M. W.
Edinburgh, 1990

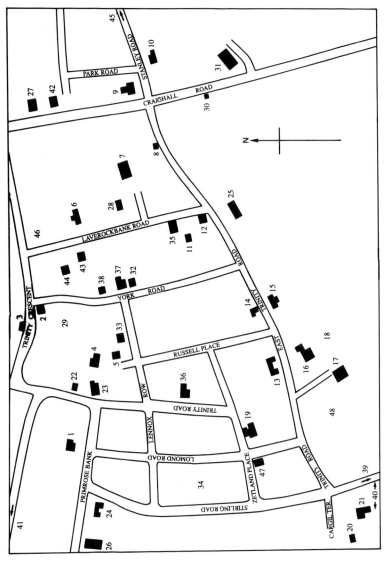

Location map of Trinity, based on map of 1894.

All Street Names

1. Shirley Lodge, formerly Primrose Bank House
2. Beach House and Bath House
3. Chain Pier Inn
4. North Trinity House
5. Gothic Cottages
6. Starbank Park and House
7. Site of Laverockbank House
8. Laverockbank Cottage, formerly South Lodge of Laverockbank House
9. Site of Belvidere House
10. Eversley
11. Woodville
12. House formerly known as The Cottage
13. Hay Lodge, site of Trinity Mains Farmhouse
14. St. Marie's
15. Site of Trinity House
16. Mayfield House
17. Site of Denham Green House
18. Earl Haig Gardens
19. House formerly known as Trinity Grove
20. Cargil Court, site of Bellfield House
21. Site of Cargilfield House
22. Site of Christian Bank
23. The former Christ Church
24. Trinity Lodge

25. Site of Lixmount House
26. Wardie Church
27. Newhaven Church
28. Bankhead, formerly Mayville
29. The former Trinity Station
30. The former Newhaven Station
31. Trinity Academy
32. Gothic House
33. Grecian Cottage
34. Lomond Park
35. Site of The Grove
36. Silverton
37. Lomond House
38. Woodbine Cottage
39. (South) Trinity Road leading to Goldenacre
40. Site of West Viewfield and East Viewfield
41. Primrose Bank Road leading to Boswell Road
42. Dunforth
43. Strathavon Lodge, formerly Viewbank
44. Inverforth
45. Stanley Road leading to Newhaven Road and Hawthornvale
46. Devlin fountain
47. Site of Trinity Hut
48. Granton Telephone Exchange in Clark Road, site of Lilyput

Key to location map of Trinity

xi

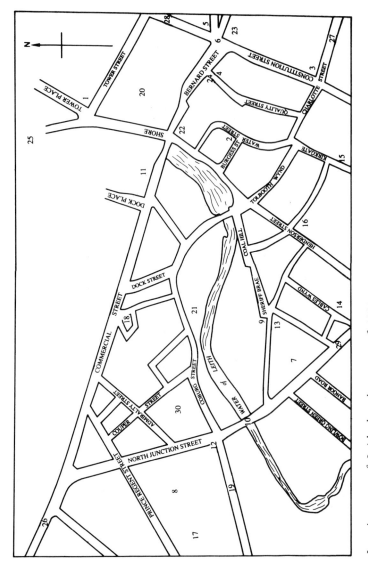

Location map of Leith, based on map of 1894

All street, river and dock names

1. Signal Tower
2. Lamb's House
3. Old Town Hall
4. Birthplace of Rev. John Home (now Maritime Street)
5. Corn Exchange
6. Burns Statue
7. Taylor Gardens, site of South Leith Poorhouse
8. Site of North Leith Poorhouse
9. The former St. Thomas's Church and Almshouses
10. Junction Bridge
11. Custom House
12. Leith Town Hall and Public Library, site of Leith Mount
13. Leith Hospital
14. Yardheads leading to St. Mary's Workshops, formerly Yardheads School
15. Kirkgate leading to Trinity House and South Leith Church
16. The Vaults
17. Madeira Street leading to North Leith Church
18. Site of Citadel (entrance arch still standing)
19. Ferry Road leading to North Fort Street and site of Leith Fort
20. Site of Timber Bush
21. North Leith Burial Ground from 1664 when Citadel built on site of original
22. The King's Wark
23. Leith Exchange and Assembly Rooms
24. The former Bank of Leith
25. Victoria Swing Bridge
26. Lindsay Road leading to Anchorfield and Newhaven
27. (Queen) Charlotte Street leading to Leith Links
28. Constitution Street leading to former Leith terminus of "Innocent" railway at Dock entrance
29. Great Junction Street leading to Junction Road Church and to Queen Victoria Statue at foot of Leith Walk
30. Couper Street School

Key to location map of Leith

Red brick and half-timbered houses built in 1920 in Primrose Bank Road. An example of good early 20th century architecture in Trinity.

CHAPTER 1

Houses in and near Trinity

A walk through Trinity, with its many quiet and seques-
tered streets and its abundant trees, reveals the diversity
and elegance of the late eighteenth-, nineteenth- and early
twentieth-century houses built in this western outlier of
Leith on the north side of the City of Edinburgh. Never a
village, the area (once part of North Leith and marked on
some maps as West Leith) began as a place of weekend, or

A view of Wardie Bay beyond the Devlin fountain in Starbank Park.

summer, residential coastal resort, and grew gradually,
around the farm of Trinity Mains, into a dormitory suburb

1

Trinity House in East Trinity Road immediately prior to demolition in 1978.

drawing its population from the Old and New Towns south of the Water of Leith but also, and principally, from the Port of Leith itself.

In the heart of Trinity, the individually designed but wholly harmonising dwellings on the northern side of East Trinity Road, with their old, mature walls and gardens, provide a satisfying and memorable visual experience in sharp contrast to that of their modern neighbours across the street. There, on the southern side, the former Trinity House, a central block of two storeys with two-storeyed flanking wings, and its garden were replaced in 1978 by several new streets, one of them approached through the entrance arches to the demolished residence. Also on the south side and a little further west is Earl Haig Gardens, a

Earl Haig Gardens, the First World War Ex-Servicemen's Settlement behind East Trinity Road.

First World War Ex-Servicemen's Settlement, in the access road to which further houses have, even more recently, been built and given the old name of Trinity Mains. This applied originally to the farm set up at this point on the Wardie Muir by the Masters and Mariners of Trinity House of Leith who, in 1713, had bought the land from the Bailiff of Queen Anne, the reigning monarch, and it was here that the district of Trinity was later to develop and extend outwards across the moor. The farmhouse of Trinity Mains was superseded by the house known as Hay Lodge and the twentieth-century houses of that name which were built when it too was taken down mark the place where the Mariners' farmhouse stood.

The modern street-name of Trinity Mains at the entrance to Earl Haig Gardens recalls the old farm of that name which stood here before the development of Trinity.

Trinity House of Leith, in the Kirkgate opposite the Parish Church of South Leith, had been dedicated, in accordance with prevailing medieval practice, to the Holy Trinity, and from it the farm and the subsequent residential area took their names. The moor itself, in the hereditary possession of the Abbots of Holyrood, had been acquired from them in 1505 by James IV to create, for shipbuilding purposes, Newhaven Harbour, and his famous ship of war, the *Great Michael*, was then constructed where the mid-nineteenth century harbour walls stand today immediately to the east of Trinity.

A cobbled pathway once led down, by the side of Trinity House, to the stables of W.T. Dunbar & Sons Ltd, the funeral directors, at No 101 East Trinity Road where

St. Marie's in East Trinity Road was built in 1823 on ground feued from the Trinity Mains farmland.

the hearses decked, like the horses that drew them, with black plumes of tall, waving feathers were a common sight in Victorian and Edwardian times as they went about their mournful missions. Garages took the place of the stables in due course but Dunbars did not leave until the 1960s when the property, including Trinity House, was bought by the House of Fraser by whom it was finally sold to a developer.

Of the Georgian houses on the north side of the street the most beautiful is St. Marie's (though it was called Mary Cottage when first built), its rear elevation bearing a strong resemblance to Laverockbank Cottage, the lodge of the demolished Laverockbank House and now a private dwelling, with its rounded stair tower and little iron balcony on top. In 1823 George Gunn, a builder, feued

The rear view of St. Marie's showing projecting stair tower with iron balcony.

the ground, which formed part of the West Tower Park, from a lawyer called Alexander Scot of Trinity Mains, on which to build the villa which was sold the following year to its first owner, William Paterson. The two-storeyed house has a dormer-windowed attic floor which is reached by a secondary stair, so typical of its period, concealed behind a door. It is probable that George Gunn, who was certainly a speculative builder, was responsible for other houses in Trinity as well and so did much to give the area its present-day appearance. Ten years later, along with George Gunn, Jnr, an engineer, he appears to have been resident at Trinity Mains himself.

On the eastern side of the villa is a stable for a single horse, but the most interesting discovery here was the

Silverton, a large Victorian villa with statutory tower built for a Leith merchant in 1865.

twenty-foot-deep, stone-lined well, which widens towards the bottom and is fed by an underground stream, which was unexpectedly revealed when a flagstone was lifted in the garden. It is to be hoped that this was not the only water supply for Mr Paterson and his family as it tends to dry up in summer. Such wells were common features in the gardens of large and even moderately sized contemporary houses. The well has been given an iron grille and a little enclosing wall has been built around it with stones from a low wall taken down in the garden. At the front, Jargonelle pear trees still climb across the walls at either side of the Ionic-columned doorway which can just be seen through the foliage behind the iron railings and at the gate.

Newbank Lodge, a former coach house, has now been converted into an attractive dwellinghouse in South Trinity Road. It is seen here behind the modern housing of Rose Park.

In Trinity Road, to the north of Birnam Lodge shaded by trees on its corner site and of similar date, is the distinctive villa called Silverton which, like Mary Cottage, was feued from the farmland of Trinity Mains. With its gables, bay windows and tall, open-topped gazebo tower, it was built in 1865 for the Leith merchant William Laing in a style which, in size and impressive, pretentious flourish, typifies the solidity and substance of Victorian Edinburgh. The sea-facing tower enabled its merchandising owner to view the progress of shipping on the Firth of Forth, and the dimensions of the rooms were planned for formal entertainment in a grand and stylish manner.

Too large for late twentieth-century living patterns, the

Larkfield Lodge stood at the Wardie Road entrance to Larkfield House in the grounds of the former Trinity Cottage at Goldenacre. Both buildings have now been demolished.

house has been divided into three, two flats at ground level and another on the floor above, while a block of fifteen further flats has been built alongside within the garden. One of Trinity's many 'tower houses', created for the southern view back to the Old Town skyline as well as for the splendid prospect of the Firth, Silverton has been adapted to meet the requirements of the present day and its new occupants can enjoy the opulent features of the interior in the knowledge that they look out on a seascape which remains unchanged (so far at least) from the day when William Laing and his family became the proud owners of their newly-built suburban home more than a hundred years ago.

Larkfield Court, the recently erected block of flats on the site of the former Larkfield Lodge.

Further down Trinity Road, and closer to the sea, is a house which was designed for himself by the architect John Dick Peddie (1824-91) in 1858. This is the now subdivided North Trinity House, a large, many-gabled and chimneyed Victorian pile standing among trees and testifying to its architectural origins with the monogram PK for the firm of Peddie & Kinnear upon the walls. Behind, at the foot of Russell Place, are North Gothic Cottage, Gothic Cottage and South Gothic Cottage, of early nineteenth-century date, and it was here that the stables of North Trinity House were located, North Gothic Cottage being incorporated for that purpose within the North Trinity House grounds by the still surviving wall with a gate-piered rear entrance from

Denham Green House, latterly the Junior Preparatory School of the Edinburgh Academy, was demolished in 1987.

Russell Place. Among the 'Gothic' features of the Cottages are pairs of small, narrow windows with pointed arches. On the corner, immediately to the south of North Trinity House, is the former Christ Church (now a house) and to its immediate north stood the long-since demolished Christian Bank which had been built in 1768.

The former eighteenth-century mansion of Rose Park lay on the west side of the present South Trinity Road. In the 1830s and '40s it was the home of George Dunbar, a professor of Greek, and the last occupants were Joseph C. Lennie, of Messrs E. & J. Lennie, Opticians at 46 Princes Street, and his family. On the death of the last Miss Lennie the whole property was sold by auction on behalf of her executors and bought for housebuilding purposes, after which the mansion was pulled down in 1962.

Newbank Lodge (so called in its own title deeds) is the name of the Rose Park coach-house off South Trinity Road which, together with the stables, survived the demolition of Rose Park itself. These two ancillary buildings have recently been restored as dwellinghouses when Newbank Lodge was found to be of brick construction, an unusual building material at that time in Scotland. The original slates are still on the roof and there is a small moulded cornice in the one public room downstairs where there are also a bedroom and a cloakroom. On the upper floor are two further bedrooms, both lit by semi-dormer windows, a modernised bathroom and generous cupboard accommodation. An interesting feature of the house is at the point of junction of the east and north walls (the building itself is set at an angle) which has been deeply cut away to form a bevelled corner. This was often the method adopted, where space was restricted, to enable a carriage, which would otherwise have struck the jutting edge of wall, to be brought round. The tarmacadam here was removed to reveal the original cobbles, so necessary for the hooves of horses, but it has been replaced in the interests of the motor car.

A larger house has been created in the stable building which, being probably older than the coach-house, is built of stone. Both are now white-harled and form an attractive group well worth the work of preservation.

The explanation of the name of the coach-house no doubt lies in the fact that another house, known as Newbank, stood somewhat south-east of Rose Park in South Trinity Road, and it is possible that a coachman was 'shared' by the owners of the two houses.

Newbank, originally known as Summerfield House, was built about 1825 by the architect David Paton for George Fulton, a teacher who wrote a number of school textbooks. David Paton, who later settled in America, was the son of John Paton, an Edinburgh builder, and both

Late 20th century housing on the site of the former Denham Green House.

father and son worked extensively in the New Town, the latter mainly during the 1820s. The villa, long since demolished, stood to the north of the now disused railway line, and two bungalows, North Newbank (also demolished) and the still extant Newbank South, were built at a later date. The Newbank site was occupied for many years by a garage and filling station which was replaced in the mid-1980s by flats and sheltered housing. In the middle of the present century the garage was owned by Thomas Fulton of R. Fulton & Co, general and motor engineers at Newbank Garage and also at No 127 Trinity Road, while North Newbank was occupied by John L. Fulton. It would thus appear (assuming the names are not coincidental) that the Fulton connection with Newbank lasted for the greater part of a hundred and fifty years, although the house must have been let at the beginning of the present century when it was occupied by the son of Sir Richard Mackie, three times Provost of the port of Leith, and by others also.

On the railway side, the masonry of Newbank South, including the two chimneys, seems to be of much earlier construction than the rest of the bungalow and it is therefore probable that some original stonework was incorporated into it at the time of building.

Immediately to the north, beside the long and narrow path that led formerly to the mansion of Rose Park and now leads to Newbank Lodge and the converted stables, the twin gate-piers, left standing after Rose Park had been taken down, have now been removed; but the two stones bearing the words 'Rose Park' in white paint were rescued and retained and have now been set up as a base for a round container, in which spring flowers and heathers have been planted, within the flat-and-sheltered-housing area on the Newbank site which has been given the old name of Rose Park. The site of the original Rose Park and its garden is now covered by Trinity Court, entered from Wardie Road from which the back of Newbank Lodge can be seen at the eastern extremity of Trinity Court.

On the southern side of the railway line, at Goldenacre, the late nineteenth-century Trinity Cottage and the older house called Larkfield were both demolished to make room for Trinity Park House, a sprawling office complex, in 1969. The lodge at the Wardie Road entrance gates to Larkfield appeared to have been spared and was permitted to house an architectural practice for some years. The environmental variety created by its black and white half-timbered, English-style design, however, along with a mature garden, have now been lost as well and a modern block of flats, called, predictably, Larkfield Court, has risen in their place.

The junior department of The Edinburgh Academy

Preparatory School having vacated Denham Green House, the Georgian villa (in which the Earl of Caithness lived in the 1830s and which had become partially concealed by later additions) was taken down in 1987 prior to the commencement of building operations on the site and in the green and pleasant ground at the corner of Clark Road and East Trinity Road which are now covered by high-density housing. Opposite Denham Green House, where the Granton telephone exchange stands today, was the little mid-eighteenth century villa, or 'hut', known as Lilliput (but shown on some old maps as Lilypot) in which dwelt the French dancing master (and keen Trinity gardener) Pierre de la Motte. The name was also used for a little street which once ran north from Ferry Road behind the house of Bangholm Bower and was called Lilypot Avenue. The two new streets have been named Caithness Place and Lilypot

Next door, on the northern side, to Woodville in Laverockbank Road stood a house, demolished after the Second World War, called The Grove. The small modern dwellings of Roseville Gardens, perhaps too close a neighbour to the old house of Woodville, were then built on the site of The Grove and its garden. The last occupants were a family called Lorimer who owned the Trinity Laundry in Hawthornvale to the east of Stanley Road.

Woodbine Cottage in York Road, its smugglers' passage to the shore now inaccessible, was built not in the eighteenth but in the early nineteenth century. This lovely little Georgian dwelling has a literary connection in the person of James Browne, LLD, the author of a *History of the Highland Clans*. He was Macvey Napier's collaborator in the *Encyclopedia Britannica*, editor of *The Edinburgh Weekly Journal* and also of *The Caledonian Mercury* a Tory newspaper which was first brought out in April 1720. (The Whig *Edinburgh Courant* began two years earlier.) In 1867 the *Caledonian Mercury* was taken over by the proprietors of *The Scotsman* and its name

Pilrig House as it appears today. After a long and eventful history it was finally rebuilt as flats in 1986.

was used for a time as a sub-title for their weekly publication. Having endeared itself to several generations of readers, it had been affectionately known as 'Granny Mercury'.

In 1829 James Browne had a difference of opinion with Mr Charles Maclaren, the then editor of the *Scotsman*, concerning a fine-art criticism. This argument was carried to such lengths that a duel took place between them near the district of Ravelston during which, however, they both avoided injuring one another. Browne died, according to James Grant, at Woodbine Cottage, Trinity, on the 8th of April 1841 aged fifty years.

No 12 Park Road is a two-storeyed Georgian villa with its chimneys, flanking two wide-spaced dormer windows, above the gables. It is set well back within its garden and is older than the rest of its neighbours in Park Road. At the north-west angle of Park Road, in its own extensive grounds, is Dunforth, now a Church of Scotland Children's Home, which was built about 1860. Prior to the Second World War this house was in the possession of Henry Robb of Henry Robb Ltd, Shipbuilders in the Port, destined to be the last survivor of the great Leith shipyards and not to close down till 1983.

The three-storey flats called Belvedere Park at the corner of Park Road and Stanley Road were built on the site of the former Belvedere House, No 24 Stanley Road, in 1978. Belvedere belonged to Mr John M. Archer, CBE, the son of Gilbert, later Sir Gilbert, Archer, JP (1882- 1948), well known as a merchant in Leith and a prominent Edinburgh citizen. St. Ola on the opposite south-east corner was owned by Sir Gilbert and bequeathed by him to the Salvation Army. His father was Registrar for South Leith as was also, it is interesting to note, his grandfather, Mr. Gilbert Archer.

Sir Gilbert was born at No. 2 Wellington Place, Leith on 6th January 1882 and died on 25th January 1948 at St. Ola after a life of outstanding public service. He was educated at Leith High School and George Heriot's, was knighted in 1942 and held office in many spheres of influence, principally as chairman of Leith Hospital Board, President of Duke Street EU Congregational Church, Master of the Merchant Company (1930-32), President of Edinburgh Chamber of Commerce (1939-41), District Commissioner for Civil Defence for South-East Scotland (1941-44) and Chairman of Leith Harbour and Dock Commission (1945-47).

On the west side of Newhaven Road the upper floor of Willowbank, its chimney-topped gables set traditionally at right angles to the street, can be seen above the garden wall. On the opposite side is the semi-detached, two-storeyed villa known as Jessfield, the most interesting of the houses at the eastern extremity of Trinity. It was built, c. 1818, as an administrative office (later converted to a house) for the naval commanding officer of the nearby Admiralty House, a building which stood in the south-west corner of the Fishermen's Park. The park is no longer in existence and Admiralty House was demolished in the 1930s to provide a site for the large, red tenements of Jessfield Terrace at the top of Whale Brae, a steep continuation of Newhaven Road into which it has since been incorporated. Jessfield House has a single dormer window, corresponding to that on the adjoining house, to the front, a cobbled courtyard recalling the days of horse-drawn carriages to the rear, and a large pentagonal conservatory.

Primrose Bank House (c. 1750 with later additions), now known as Shirley Lodge, in Primrose Bank Road was the Newhaven Manse at the end of the nineteenth century.

The strangely-named Taap Hall (No 219 Ferry Road) was owned by a Dutch shipmaster in Leith called Thomas Taap and it carries its identification, along with its building date of 1790, above the door. There is also a tradition, however, that the present building replaced the shipmaster's early nineteenth-century villa which had been built on the site of a previous house. The large and pleasing tenement stands behind an equally pleasing front garden and its plain stone walls rise to three storeys and extend across seven bays. It is still, as flats, in residential occupation.

Also in Ferry Road, and next door on the western side to Bonnington Bank House, is Laurel Bank (No 211), a plain Georgian villa with a projecting porch, a Victorian addition on the east side, a forecourt with sheltering trees to the front and a walled garden at the back.

A number of old and interesting houses could once have been found in the district of Bonnington but hardly any have survived, most of them following the usual road to ruin beginning with the death or departure of their owners and the use of the buildings and grounds for purposes detrimental to their preservation, and ending with their sites being taken over for street and tenement building. Such was the case with the manorhouse of Bonnington itself. It stood at the junction of Graham Street and West Bowling Green Street which were laid out after its demolition and which, in their turn, have now largely disappeared, taking with them the one remaining lodge which survived for a time at the south-west corner of Graham Street. Still on the ground today is a single reminder of the vanished Bonnington estate—a long, two-storey Georgian cottage at No 176 Newhaven Road next door to the former Bonnington Academy at No 174. It lies obliquely within a sloping garden and has a white-painted ironwork balcony above the door. The first mansionhouse (it was later rebuilt) was erected around 1630 and the second vanished from the scene, much altered and extended, in the 1890s.

After several occupants, including the descendants of the Crawfords of Bonnington who owned the lands in the sixteenth century, had come and gone the house was bought, in 1717, by Thomas Brown, the Edinburgh publisher and bookseller, who made several alterations to the building. A subsequent owner was the advocate James Clerk, a connection of the Clerks of Penicuik and the son of John Clerk, an eighteenth-century President of the Royal College of Physicians in Edinburgh. James Clerk, who had purchased the lands and mansion in 1786, married a daughter of Thomas Rattray, DD, of Craighall near Blairgowrie, and changed his name to Clerk-Rattray. Craighall Road in Trinity was so called from his estate in Perthshire (though it had at first been known, and even marked on maps, as the New Cut because it provided a more direct access to Newhaven), and it was from one of his descendants that the ground in Craighall Road on which Trinity Academy was built by the Leith School Board was bought in 1888.

By the time the Clerk-Rattrays acquired it the old house had been let, the first tenant, in 1782, being Major Henry

Sir Gilbert Archer, well known for his outstanding public service prior to and during the Second World War, was born in Leith and resided and died in Trinity. (Photograph by courtesy of Gilbert B. Archer, Esq.).

Balfour who chose it as a residence because Pilrig House, in which he had been born, could be seen from its windows. After his death in 1787 the house, wrote John Russell, 'declined in status' and the lands grew gradually smaller as a result of feuing. Suffering the same fate as Stewartfield, Bonnington House became a dairy, its grounds having been taken over and used as nurseries, prior to its demolition.

The last laird of Pilrig was John Mackintosh Balfour-Melville. In 1883, as Mr Balfour, he had succeeded as heir of entail to the estate of Mount Melville, near St. Andrews in Fife, and added that name to his own. Beginning to feu his land at the top of the avenue which led to Leith Walk (the present Balfour Street), he started the tenement building which was soon to proliferate in the area. On his death in 1893 his brother inherited Mount Melville and his unmarried daughters, the Misses Balfour-Melville, came to live—the last of their family to do so—in Pilrig House. After years of neglect the old mansion, with its memories of Robert Louis Balfour Stevenson, was rebuilt as flats in 1986.

The Stewarts who gave their name to Stewartfield, having come to Edinburgh from Perthshire, bought their Bonnington acres, which had been detached from the estate of Pilrig a few years earlier, in 1746, and in 1813 they were sold to Hugh Veitch, Town Clerk of Leith and grandfather of the First World War General, Earl Haig. The mid-eighteenth century house of Stewartfield was let as an hotel in 1855 and the grounds became for a time, again in the words of John Russell, 'a kind of Vauxhall Gardens'. In 1895, after it had served as a dairy farm for almost twenty years, the Caledonian Railway Company purchased the estate and demolished the mansionhouse. The old walls of Stewartfield extended from Bonnington Toll northwards to the mills of Bonnington on the west side of Newhaven Road. The name of the house has recently been given to a group of workshop units erected here under the Leith project umbrella, a scheme which has now instilled much-needed new life into the Port.

During the 1780s the old Whiting Road, which was merely a country track, was transformed into a carriageway and called Bonnington Road, a name it retained until, in the 1860s, the present Bonnington Road was constructed when it became, and has remained, Newhaven Road. At the same time a lodge and new entrance gates to Bonnington Park House were built, access having formerly been obtained from Ferry Road. The house is now known as Victoria Park House and took its present name from Victoria Park which was laid out in its grounds in 1919. John Cundell, who had bought part of the lands of Bonnington, was the builder of Bonnington Park House and it was here that he died in 1810. The house, which has seen many alterations and extensions, passed towards the end of the century to Richard Raimes of Raimes Clark & Co Ltd, the manufacturing chemists at Nos 17 and 19 Smith's Place, and when Victoria Park was opened it was known locally as Raimes Park while the old name was still remembered. The last occupants of Bonnington Park, during the First World War, were William Inglis, of John Inglis & Sons Ltd, corn millers in Bonnington, and his family and, after its purchase by the Town Council, the mansionhouse, No 161 Newhaven Road, took on its present role of a Child Welfare Home.

In 1929 Sir Robert Lorimer converted the villa on the east side of Warriston Road behind Warriston Cemetery called East Warriston House to its present function as a crematorium. The architect of this once-attractive Georgian house has not yet been traced but his client was Andrew Bonar, the banker, of Ramsay, Bonar & Co, one of several Edinburgh banking houses that helped to finance the ambitious New Town building operations in progress when, in 1808, the villa was built. (The building date for this house is usually given as 1818 but recent research has proved this to be erroneous.) Horatius Bonar, the well-known hymn writer, was a nephew of the original owner. (West Warriston House, demolished in the 1960s, was in Inverleith Row.)

Of several Georgian villas built in the vicinity of Leith Links, Prospect Bank House, now No 16 Prospect Bank Road, alone survives. Of eighteenth-century date and painted white, it consists of two storeys above a basement, across which it is entered by a short flight of steps, and two single-storey wings.

On the western edges of Trinity, where Granton Road meets Wardie Crescent, is the house called Grantons. Designed by the architect David Bryce, its date of building, 1855, is incorporated in the carving on the lintel-stone above the door. This large, ornate, typically Victorian and

The Cottage, facing East Trinity Road, was the Edinburgh home of the actor, Frank Worthing. Photograph c. 1898.

now divided dwelling is shown on early twentieth-century maps as Granton Villa, but its later name of Grantons can be seen on both gatepiers at the now blocked-up carriage entrance on the corner.

At the junction of East Trinity and Laverockbank Roads are the converted flats No 50 East Trinity Road (upper flat) and No 16 Laverockbank Road (lower flat). Before the Second World War this house was known as The Cottage but it started life about the year 1816 as a true single-storey cottage (in early directories it is given simply as 'cottage') and was not extended by a staircase and a second storey till late in the nineteenth century. Its name changed with the years also, being first Spring Cottage, then Ramsay Cottage and finally The Cottage.

Ramsay Cottage, as it then was, was the home of the Rev George R. Davidson from 1876 - 77 and Mr J.C. Deans from 1886-87. It had become The Cottage by the time it was occupied by Mr W.A. Young from 1889-90 and in the latter year (probably the year in which it was enlarged to become a villa) it was bought by Mr Young Johnston Pentland, the owner of a cooperage, Y.J. Pentland & Son, Coopers and Stave Merchants, in Spence's Place (later to become part of Bonnington Road) in Leith, a family business which had been founded by his father, also called Young Johnston Pentland, who was born in 1798 and who, along with his wife, is buried in the graveyard of South Leith Church, the place being marked by a white marble tablet on the wall. No-one now knows why such an unusual Christian name was given to several generations of sons who, even in old age, were still addressed as Young. They had removed from Muirville (his wife's maiden name was Muir) in Newhaven Road opposite Victoria Park, Muirville being now a home for the elderly belonging to the Baptist Church.

The Pentlands had fourteen children, so large a tribe, in fact, that they called their parents 'the Father' and 'the Mother' and when they went to the West Coast for their annual holiday each summer it became increasingly difficult to rent a house which was big enough to accommodate them all. The story has come down that two of the boys had once to sleep in a tiny attic where they found they had to do everything in turns because, in order to stand upright, they were obliged to put their heads out of the skylight window—one at a time! Most of the children were sent to Mr Hunter's Bonnington Academy in Newhaven Road, the boys going later to the Royal High School in Edinburgh.

Like all Victorian families, they created their own entertainment and were much given to dressing up and acting, and one of them, Francis George Pentland (born in 1866 and the proverbial seventh son) showed promise of theatri-

Frank Worthing was the original Lieut. Pinkerton in *Madam But-terfly* when the play was first produced in New York in 1900. He is seen here with the American actress Blanche Bates in the title role.

cal ability above the average and was destined to rise to prominence, at the turn of the century, on the American stage.

Intended by his parents for a career in medicine, this was soon abandoned in favour of his own strong predilection for a life on the boards. Never physically robust, he joined the Edinburgh Dramatic Society in his high-spirited and inexperienced youth but was never again to act in his native city. Shortly afterwards, Walter Hatton of the Edinburgh Theatre Royal obtained for him the job of assistant prompter and player of small parts at fifteen shillings a week in a repertory company at South Shields and, once there, he was soon being given more important roles. After playing supporting parts in several companies he went to Worthing to study dramatic art, and it was while he was there that he decided upon a change of name. His brother, David Nicol Pentland, was also on the stage and so, to avoid confusion, he emerged as a professional actor who was from then on known to the public as Frank Worthing. In 1888, at the age of twenty-two, he made his debut on the London stage. The critics were kind and acclaimed him as a rising star but noted signs of the nervous agitation which he was never able wholly to overcome throughout the rest of his life.

In 1890 Mrs Patrick Campbell was looking for a leading man to play Orlando to her Rosalind in *As You Like It* at the Shaftesbury Theatre, and her choice fell upon the young Scottish actor who afterwards made several appearances with this celebrated actress. Then Mrs Lily Langtry, her company about to go on tour, asked Frank to join her, and with her he portrayed a series of characters including Marc Anthony, Pygmalion in *Pygmalion and Galetea* and Charles Surface in Sheridan's *The School for Scandal*, a part he was to play often in the future and which soon became his favourite role. After that came work with one of Henry Irving's companies, followed by a contract with Charles Wyndham to play at the Criterion Theatre.

About this time the actress Olga Nethersole was going out to join Augustin Daly's company in New York and she suggested to him that he might not be averse to taking on a leading man from the English stage as well. He was not, and in 1894, at the age of twenty-eight, Frank Worthing made the first of his many Atlantic crossings. There now began a period of high-intensity work and travel, in which he played a wide variety of parts from Shakespeare to the popular drawing-room farces of the day and the light comedy in which he particularly excelled, which was to last for his remaining sixteen years of life. He was tall and distinctive in appearance with a deep, musical voice, very large blue eyes of unusual mobility and an exceptional memory, while his animated manner, heightened by a large measure of the individualistically 'Pentland' sense of humour, was balanced by a strong and sensitive personality. From now on he played opposite the leading ladies of the American stage, was recalled to England by Mrs Patrick Campbell to act opposite her during a London season, took the part of Armand Duval in *Camille —The Lady of the Camellias*—and, in 1900, was the original Lieut Pinkerton in *Madam Butterfly*, the dramatic production on which Puccini subsequently based his opera, written in 1904.

Frank made New York, where a married sister and one of his married brothers were also living, his American base and took an apartment overlooking Central Park. But there were many hurried homecomings to The Cottage in Trinity and each summer it rang with the transatlantic accents of visiting theatrical celebrities, one of whom presented Mr and Mrs Pentland with his water-colour painting of the house and garden in 1898. All the family bore a strong resemblance to both their parents as, in addition to being his second wife, 'the Mother' of the fourteen children had married her cousin!

It was when Frank Worthing was in San Francisco with the Daly company in 1896 that the shadow of tragedy began to fall across his life. Mr Daly had engaged an aspiring young actress from New England called Maxine Elliott (whose sister Gertrude was later to marry the outstanding English actor Johnston Forbes-Robertson) and Frank was immediately asked to play opposite to her in several productions. Falling quickly and deeply in love with her, he had at first every reason to believe she returned his affections, and soon the other members of the company were expecting the announcement of their engagement. Daly now took them all to England to fulfil a short engagement and Maxine and Frank went everywhere together as he showed her, pleased and excited by her first visit there, the sights of London.

Back in the States, they were co-starred in a play called *The Two Escutcheons* when the season opened, but before long Nat Goodwin, the most celebrated comedian of the day in the American theatre, arrived in San Francisco and it was not long before his interest was aroused by the raven-haired beauty of Maxine Elliott. Recklessly, Nat Goodwin decided upon a plundering action: he would take her from both Frank Worthing and Augustin Daly, and he made a sudden offer to Maxine of a place in his company and an immediate voyage to Australia which she, equally suddenly, accepted. As the news spread among the cast it was accompanied by a whispered understanding that Frank had fainted when he heard of it. Maxine Elliott's eventual marriage to Nat Goodwin ended in divorce and, leaving the stage, she went on to become a glittering society hostess in London and Europe and to count King Edward VII and Noel Coward among her friends.

For Frank Worthing it was a very different story. With redoubled effort he plunged into work even more exhaustingly and was soon neglecting himself and eating little. Two years later he had to be assisted from the stage during a performance and before long was concealing from the outside world, and probably, at times, even from himself, that he had consumption. In 1908 he was taken to hospital with pneumonia and his manager was told that in all probability he would never act again. Retirement from the theatre was urged upon him but he would not hear of it, though the consequences must have been clear to him now and had no doubt been clear enough well before his illness which, prophetically, had overtaken him in Detroit in Michigan.

After a quiet and prolonged vacation Frank Worthing embarked for a homeward voyage and his annual visit to The Cottage where he maintained his usual reticence about his health. Not for nothing, however, was he called by those who knew him best in the States 'the stubborn Scot' and, somewhat revived by the invigorating summer winds of the Firth of Forth at Trinity, he responded at once when a cable was delivered to The Cottage requesting his 'immediate return, if willing, for an engagement'. He went back on the *Lusitania*, that ill-fated ship which, seven years

This photograph of Frank Worthing was reproduced in the *Leith Observer* in January 1911 after his death in the United States.

later, was to be sunk by a German torpedo and so to precipitate the entrance of the United States into the First World War.

The last play in which Frank Worthing acted was a comedy called *Sauce for the Goose* by Geraldine Bonnar in which he played opposite Grace George, the American actress. The production was taken on tour at the end of December 1910 and was due to open at the Garrick Theatre in Detroit on the 26th. The weather was cold and he had a severe haemorrhage from the lungs before leaving New York. The strain of the first night telling heavily on his strength, Grace George tried to persuade him to allow an understudy to take his part the following day, but he refused to give in. Reaching the stage door on the evening of the 27th Frank could get no further. He collapsed just inside the theatre and was soon unconscious. Some time later an announcement was made to the waiting audience: 'Mr Worthing's sudden illness appears critical. In consequence the performance will be cancelled', and twenty minutes later he was dead. Frank had wanted to die in harness and at the age of forty-four his wish was granted.

Slowly and quietly the theatre was vacated, and in the silence that followed Grace George led the rest of the cast onto the stage. For two hours they sat amongst the scenery set up for the abandoned comedy performance, their subdued voices echoing faintly in the empty auditorium as they recalled Frank's career in England and America, his lavish prodigality of his brittle strength, and now his last untimely but characteristic exit from the stage. 'I cannot undertake the part tomorrow night', said Grace as she left the theatre.

On December 30th 1910 a funeral service was held at 'The Little Church Around the Corner' in New York, a place of worship which the acting profession had made its own, after which Frank was buried in the Greenwood Cemetery in Brooklyn, on Long Island, in a burial plot belonging to the members of the Pentland family in New York.

His death was widely reported in the American press and his photograph, along with an outline of his career, was published in the *Leith Observer* of 7th January 1911 which offered sympathy to his relatives, 'still resident in this burgh', in their bereavement. An illustrated book on Frank Worthing's life, with a repertory of some two hundred of his multiplicity of parts, was published by The Lambs, a theatrical club in New York of which, as well as of The Players, he had been a member. In addition to acting, he had written, anonymously, several one-act plays which were performed for benefits and to provide work for struggling actors, but none has survived as, believing their purpose to have been served, he destroyed them all himself. Along with those of other members of his family, his name can still be read, with the place and date of

The Pentland burial plot and obelisk (centre) in Rosebank Cemetery.

death, on the tall, grey granite monumental obelisk in Rosebank Cemetery, not far from Laverockbank, at Bonnington.

In 1988 it was discovered that an English lady, who went to London frequently to attend theatrical performances, idolised Frank Worthing as an actor. Coming to Edinburgh on her marriage, she stayed in an East Trinity Road flat the windows of which overlooked the garden of The Cottage immediately opposite. Years after his death she spoke about him to her daughters but, unaware of his real name, never knew of his Edinburgh origins or that it was his family who lived directly across the street from her own home!

The Pentlands, their numbers slowly but steadily in decline, continued to reside in the burgh until just before the Second World War. The parents celebrated their golden wedding in The Cottage in 1905, but by then 'the Mother' was frail and ageing and she died soon afterwards. Young Johnston, now a widower for the second time, followed her to their Rosebank resting place eleven months later at the age of seventy-eight, both having been spared the sorrow of Frank's early death. The cooperage was wound up a few years later, by that time in the hands of Young Johnston Pentland the third. David Pentland had never had the theatrical success of his brother and by 1933, when he too died in The Cottage, the house had become run down and permeated by dampness from the deep-rooted ivy that had now spread, unchecked, across the walls till it covered the stonework and kept the daylight from the windows. One by one death removed the remaining unmarried brothers and sisters until, in 1938, the last one was gone. The garden, already reduced in size by a recent widening of the pavement, was neglected and overgrown. Later that year The Cottage was sold to a building contractor, but because of the outbreak of war a few months afterwards all work on the property had to be postponed, and it sank into abandonment and gloom. Around 1943 the staircase collapsed, weakened and perished by dry rot.

Its rescuers returned in 1946, dividing it and building an outside access stair to the upper flat on the western side. They tore the ivy and virginia creeper from the walls, made a new aditional entrance in East Trinity Road and finally took away its name as well. Strangely, the house looks younger now than it did in its happy, late Victorian prime, but it keeps its memories well hidden from the public gaze.

CHAPTER 2

Housing the Homeless

BY the middle of the nineteenth century Leith, an ancient seaport with an unplanned layout of congested streets, crowded closes and deteriorated dwellings, had been reduced to a level comparable with the slum-conditions of the Old Town of Edinburgh. In earlier times the trade incorporations and craft guilds had made themselves responsible for the poor among their numbers and, after the Reformation in 1560, the kirk sessions of individual congregations took over the task of caring for the sick and the underprivileged on a parish basis. Poorhouses were, by and large, a Victorian invention (though Trinity House had proposed a poorhouse in 1749) and, although North Leith had one as early as the mid-eighteenth century, it was not till the mid-nineteenth that the much larger South Leith acquired a similar building for the reception of the homeless whose plight then, as in the past, was only relieved, when it was relieved at all, by acts of charity on the part of those who could afford them and the meagre amounts paid out by the appropriate authorities.

The poorhouses themselves provided only the most basic form of shelter and even in 1884 it was reported in Leith that their accommodation, alone in Scotland, was without any day-rooms for its inmates. By 1899, less than a hundred years ago and during the period of its independence, Leith was appealing to its old overlord, the City of Edinburgh, to take as many as one hundred destitute poor out of the burgh - and incurring the time-honoured indignation of the capital. The Leith Poorhouse, on the site of the present Taylor Gardens at the east end of Great Junction Street, was now inadequate and the port had its sights on the poorhouse at Craigleith. At a meeting of the Edinburgh Parish Council in early January, although it was decided not to sell the Craigleith Poorhouse it had nonetheless been moved 'that the Edinburgh Parish Council intimate their willingness to consider any proposal by which, subject to any required sanction of the Local Government Board, such portion as may be arranged of the Leith poor may be accommodated in Craigleith Poorhouse, thereby saving the Leith Parish Council the contemplated heavy capital expenditure for the erection of a new poorhouse. It was not too much to hope that this might bring about a solution of what had been a very troublesome question.'

By the time the next meeting was held, however, the mood had changed and the Edinburgh Council asked the proposer to withdraw his motion 'because they had quite enough to do to accommodate their own poor in the buildings they had at present.' It was contended that Craigleith did not have the capacity to take in so large a number and, in any case, it questioned whether the Edinburgh Council had power 'to let Craigleith as a common lodging-house to Leith.' It being confirmed that they had no such power unless by arrangement with Leith and subject to the consent of the Local Government Board, the conclusion was reached that 'it was not the province of the Edinburgh Parish Council to do the business of Leith, which they were capable of doing themselves if they were so minded'. In spite of so emphatic a statement of their sentiments, the motion was not withdrawn but was, paradoxically, adopted by nineteen votes to seven.

With a new century about to dawn, times were changing and Leith, after briefly entertaining the possibility of building a new poorhouse at Easter Duddingston, withdrew the subject from its deliberations. The poor law was of very ancient origin and there was every likelihood that, in the near future, it would be revised. (Ten years earlier, in 1889, there had been 51 inmates in the North House, which was by then a hospital, while those in the South House numbered 187.) The enlightened idea of building cottage homes was being suggested and the old Poorhouse was allowed to remain in existence until 1907 when it was removed to Seafield.

Provost and Mrs Malcolm Smith were philanthropic to the Seafield Poorhouse, sending a case of oranges and a barrel of apples at New Year and entertaining the inmates to a 'social'. In 1911 this consisted of tea and cakes between 6.30 and 7 pm followed by a concert, with sweets and toys for the children, who it was reported 'looked the picture of health and happiness', presented by Mrs Smith. The Provost in his remarks said that he was sure they would not object now and again to having a change from the porridge they usually got at supper, and added that, as some of them were now to qualify for a pension in place of poorhouse residence, they should consider the matter carefully as, in spite of some restriction on their movements, they were very comfortable and well looked after where they were!

The next stage was the demolition of the poorhouses and the building of slum clearance housing. The first of these 'schemes', in 1925, was in the district of Lochend to which it was intended to move the slum dwellers of the Cowgate, the Grassmarket and the Pleasance as well as Leith. It may have been taken as a foregone conclusion that this would come as welcome news to the deprived and demoralised families who were involved. But it did not, and many people from all these areas refused to be rehoused. Although the rents were to be specially reduced, the cost was still too high to be afforded, particularly when tram fares to places of work at a distance from Lochend had to be paid as well; and shopping would be more expensive too. The slum houses, however, were being condemned and the overcrowding became worse when they were closed as, rather than leave the central area of Leith, people often preferred to move in with relatives or friends who were still living in the old, familiar neighbourhoods. These changes were among the direct results of the

1920 amalgamation and the Edinburgh Town Council, faced with this unexpected situation, was uncertain as to how best to handle it.

Three-roomed houses were to be let at a rent of £15 a year and two-roomed houses at £12, but the smaller and cheaper dwellings had been built in insufficient numbers and it was therefore decided to provide them and an undertaking was given to have them ready in a few weeks' time. The others were to be allocated to ex-servicemen and their families, but even this was opposed because it would divide the community into 'sheep and goats, i.e. those who had seen military service and those who had not'. The needs of the families should be the only consideration.

Some of the rents were intended to be even higher and 'the whole question of assessing rents at Lochend was a standing disgrace', complained the *Edinburgh and Leith Observer*. It was finally agreed that, 'rather than have scores of houses ready for occupation and nobody to go into them', they would let 300 out of the 734 houses built to the slum clearance tenants who were in greatest need and would give priority to ex-servicemen as well. Those not taken up, however, were to be let to the general public at a rent of £28 for a three-roomed house. Difficulties notwithstanding, the rehousing programme went ahead and in that year, 1925, three thousand houses were either completed or were approaching completion.

Recent experiments in providing low-cost housing have in many respects been even more unsatisfactory. Thomas Fraser and John Russell Courts, built in Couper Street in the 1960s as twenty-storey towerblocks (or upended streets), created immediate problems, especially for families with very young children, and even the lower-rise buildings like Fort House with only seven storeys are depressingly institutional in character in comparison to the more human scale of houses dating from before the Second World War.

Demolition proved to be too soft an option in Leith and

the resulting gap-sites were left to disfigure the streets for many years. But now, thanks to the enthusiastic work carried out on behalf of the Leith Project and the Leith Enterprise Trust in the last few years, all that is changing. The gap-sites are disappearing and life, renewed and exuberant, is again returning to the port which is as mindful of its roots and its remaining architectural assets as it is sure of its place—and the fulfilment of its perseverance—in the future.

CHAPTER 3

Churches

THE first ecclesiastical building on the site of the present South Leith Church was begun - as the New Kirk of Our Lady - shortly after 1480 and its association with the Scottish monarchy dates from its inception, James III contributing, in 1487, to the cost of its construction. In 1559, the year before her death in Edinburgh Castle, Mary of Guise, the Queen Regent and mother of Mary Queen of Scots, worshipped in the church that was soon to suffer so severely in her defence of the Port against the Reformers and their English army. Her grandson, James VI, had an even stronger connection with the Kirk. David Lindsay, the first Protestant minister of Leith, accompanied James to Norway where he conducted the marriage ceremony of the king to Anne of Denmark in 1589, and later, in 1600, he baptised, in Dunfermline, the future King Charles I. Two silver communion cups bearing the Royal Coat-of-Arms and the date 1617 were presented to the church by James VI on his only visit to Scotland after the Union of the Crowns in 1603.

South Leith Church as it appears today is to a large extent the work of the architect Thomas Hamilton who incorporated the old structure, or what was left of it, into the new parish church in 1848, reducing the cruciform building to a nave (more suited to Presbyterian worship) and dismantling two of the four galleries which had been erected in 1609 when, by an Act of Parliament, St. Mary's had first become the Parish Church of South Leith.

Although the nave escaped serious injury in 1560, the choir and transepts had been virtually destroyed and the seventeenth century tower, surmounted by a Dutch-style

South Leith Church stands opposite Trinity House in the Kirkgate and owes its present appearance to the 19th century architect Thomas Hamilton.

wood and metal spire, was considered to be unsafe in 1836 and taken down. Along with the nave, the west window of the old church survived, and, indeed, can still be seen, though it has to be sought in another building in a most unlikely place.

During the course of the Hamilton rebuilding the window, in the Second or Decorated Gothic style, was removed and on subsequent examination there seemed to be no reason to doubt that it formed part of the original fabric. It was nevertheless replaced in the same position by a replica. The old window was then taken to the home of Dr D.H. Robertson, the author of *The Sculptured Stones of Leith* and a member of South Leith Church, at No 43 Albany Street (then beside North Fort Street but no longer in existence) where, according to a contemporary account, it was rebuilt "stone by stone" in the garden where it was to stand undisturbed for approximately seventy years.

About 1880 a Mr Walter Campbell bought from the Marquis of Breadalbane a little island in Loch Awe in Argyllshire and on it he built a mansionhouse for himself, his mother and his sister. Mrs Campbell, however, being too infirm to make a weekly journey to the parish church in Dalmally, her son decided to design and construct a place of worship for her by the lochside to be called St. Conan's Kirk. It was completed in 1886 and, although adequate for the tiny congregation it attracted, was small and unadorned, and Walter Campbell was dissatisfied with his work. Between 1907 and his death in 1914 he devoted himself to the task of enlarging and embellishing the church, and the result is a unique and interesting building. And among its great variety of features is the west window of the Kirk of Our Lady in South Leith which was taken to Argyllshire from the Albany Street garden and found, despite the passage of time, to be 'in a splendid state of preservation'. Mr Campbell, who wished to remain anonymous, gave an undertaking that he would return the window in the event of later restoration being carried out at South Leith on condition that another of similar design was substituted in the Argyll church. To this day, however, it still lights the Bruce Chapel in St. Conan's Kirk, Loch Awe.

On the completion of this transaction John Russell, the Leith historian, wrote a strong letter of protest to the *Leith Observer* lamenting the loss of the old window to the people of Leith.

In 1976 the oldest surviving tombstone in South Leith churchyard, having become buried beneath the ground, was rediscovered and brought to light. It marked the grave of Adam Abercrombie, the church's session clerk at the time of the great visitation of plague in 1645 when, as he wrote in the session minutes of that fateful year, 'the number of dead exceeded the number of living.' The outbreak had started in the King James Hospital beside the church and his records reveal the urgency with which the bailies and the South Leith elders strove to improve the insanitary conditions in the Kirkgate where an open sewer ran down the middle of the street. Abercrombie himself survived the 'peste', and died and was buried here in 1656.

In the same year repairs to the stonework of the church tower were carried out, and the clock was rejuvenated too and provided with new clock faces, recalling the vital part which the old timepiece played in the days when people depended on public clocks for the good ordering of their lives. It was the sexton's task to ring the first rising bell, for the carters, at 5.30 in the morning, and again at half past six for the mill and shipyard workers and all others who started at 7 am. In the evening the curfew bell was rung at half past eight. 'The pattern of daily bell-ringing', wrote the minister of South Leith Church in 1976 in the local newspaper, 'stopped as recently as 1939 on the outbreak of the Second World War. Church bells were to be rung after that only in the event of an invasion'.

By 1850 there was presumably no longer a clock on the South Leith tower as in May of that year the church minutes record a suggestion that the Council should put the sum of thirty pounds at the disposal of the Provost's Committee for the purpose of placing a clock in the church spire for the benefit of the town. There was some disagreement among the Councillors, however, as to whether they had sufficient funds, and the question did not arise again until September of 1851 when a proposal was made to repair the old timepiece outside the Clock Tavern at The Shore of Leith. Like all ancient clocks, it had just one hand and it was now put forward that hour and minute hands should be provided for two dials at a cost of £8.10s. or, alternatively, that a new timepiece dial and movement be installed for twelve pounds which could be kept in proper working order for an annual payment of twelve shillings. This would cover the cost of winding every week but would be reduced to six shillings 'if the parties wound it themselves'. It would not be a striking clock which was not recommended because it would be too expensive. The Council, in generous mood, decided in favour of the new movement.

There is no such street as Junction Road, but the eastern part of Great Junction Street up to the old Kirkgate was so called by popular consent and it was here, in 1825, that Junction Road Secession Church was built. Some years afterwards, in 1843, St. Thomas's Church was erected at Sheriff Brae. At that time the possibility that these two congregations would ever unite would have seemed remote, but Secession churches having, by way of United Presbyterian and United Free amalgamations, re-entered the fold of the established church, that union was to take place in 1975 at a time of even more unexpected developments at Sheriff Brae.

The building of St. Thomas's Church necessitated the demolition of an ancient mansion which stood, facing Coalhill, at the head of Sheriff, or Shirra, Brae. This house, according to tradition, was the home of 'Tibbie Fowler o' the Glen', celebrated in Scottish song as the lass 'carried off', despite the 'ane and forty wooing her', by one of the notorious Logans of Restalrig. He must have taken over the mansionhouse as well as in 1572 it was in the possession of 'Majestro Joanne Logan de Shireff Braye'. The dormer windows were elegantly carved, one with a heart surmounted by a fleur-de-lis with the date 1636 and the initials I.L. Another had a shield and the initials M.C., while the initials D.D., M.C. and the date 1730 must have been the work of a later mason. In 1840 the old house was taken down, but the sculptured stones from the dormers were preserved and built into the north wall of St. Thomas's Church Manse where they remained

The former St. Thomas's Church, now a Sikh Temple, at Sheriff Brae. On the left are the almshouses built at the same time as part of the benefaction to Leith by Sir John Gladstone of Fasque.

until that building was destroyed by fire during the First World War.

As a memorial to his family and his own connection with Leith, the church still standing at the top of Sheriff Brae was built on the site of the Logan mansion by Sir John Gladstone of Fasque, father of the Victorian statesman, who had been born in the Coalhill in 1764. He employed John Henderson, the architect of Newhaven Parish Church, to draw up plans, not only for the church itself, but also for a manse and school to the north, and a row of almshouses to the west for the accommodation of ten incurable old women. These buildings form an open courtyard to Mill Lane, on the other side of which the old Leith Hospital looks towards Great Junction Street across

Taylor Gardens laid out on the site of the former South Leith Poorhouse.

On 3rd April 1916, during a Zeppelin raid on Leith, an incendiary bomb destroyed St. Thomas's Manse, though no-one was hurt in the incident. The church was undamaged and continued in use as a place of worship until union was effected, in May 1975, with the Junction Road congregation, when the former church building was opened, on 30th June 1976, as a Sikh Temple, a role not likely to have been foreseen by John Gladstone at the time of his benefaction to Leith when the whole range of buildings had cost him the sum of ten thousand pounds.

Considerable alterations were made to part of the almshouse range when it was incorporated in a stadium and ballroom complex at the rear, and further damage was done in 1984 by a fire in which the modern complex was destroyed. An application was then made for permission to demolish the rest of the building, No 6 Mill Lane, for the purposes of house building on the site of the former stadium. The C-listed group of almshouse range and church is situated within the Old Leith Conservation Area and it was therefore recommended that the Mill Lane facade should be retained and redevelopment confined to the open ground at the back and the fire-damaged interior of the house. By 1987 no work had been carried out on the Jacobean-style asylum or almshouse buildings and, though the former St. Thomas's spire continued to dominate the Sheriff Brae, the immediate surroundings acquired a neglected and run-down appearance. During the following year, however, agreement was reached on the implementation of a conservation scheme for this group of buildings which has resulted in the environmental upgrading of this part of Leith.

The Sikh Temple was badly damaged as a consequence of deliberate fireraising on 26th May 1989.

The church in Great Junction Street, now St. Thomas-Junction Road, is still a well-preserved church building with a worshipping congregation and a purposeful part to play in the community. Within the vestibule is a fine carved marble monument commemorating The Rev Francis Muir, a well-known minister in Leith, who died in 1871. Before the amalgamation of the two churches The Rev Rudolf J. Ehrlich was the last minister of Junction Road from 1952 until his death in 1974. He was for many years a lecturer in German at New College.

The Roman Catholic Church of St. Mary's Star of the Sea stands in Constitution Street on ground that belonged to the former Balmerino House which had been built as early as 1631. It is shown in a nineteenth century print as a three-storey mansion with an ornamental, pedimented doorway, approached by a flight of steps, and a half-sunk basement, but this east-facing facade had by that time been altered and modernised.

In 1643 it was purchased from the Earl of Carrick, by whom it had been built, by John, Lord Balmerino, with whose family it remained till the mid-eighteenth century. Charles II lodged here briefly when Cromwell was attacking Edinburgh and it was the residence, during the Jacobite Rebellion of 1745, of Arthur Elphinstone, sixth Lord Balmerino, whose dedication to the lost cause of the exiled Stuarts carried him through the campaign of Prince Charles Edward to his capture after the battle of Culloden and to his execution on Tower Hill in London after which his estates were confiscated.

Following various ownerships, the house and grounds were bought for £1475 by William Sibbald, a Leith merchant, who caused the old mansion to be sub-divided and let out to tenants. In 1848, decayed and in disrepair, the ancient dwelling, with its environs, was purchased by the Roman Catholic Church who used it as a school before building the present church within its gardens. The church was enlarged in the early years of the twentieth century but all trace of Balmerino House has disappeared.

No 7 Lennox Row in Trinity, the large, gabled, sevenbedroomed Victorian house half hidden by trees on the opposite side to Grecian Cottage, a white Maltese Cross beside its gate, belonged, as St. John's Hospice, to the order of St. John in Scotland until its closure in 1987. The Knights Hospitallers, or Knights of St. John of Jerusalem, were founded at the time of the Crusades in the eleventh century. One of the three military Orders created for the protection of pilgrims to the Holy Sepulchre, it was introduced into Scotland by David I who gave them lands at Torphichen, in West Lothian, and here their curious fortified church, or Preceptory, still stands today. There are ten Scottish St. John Associations throughout the country and the Headquarters of The Priory of Scotland of the Order of St. John can be found in St. John Street on the south side of the Canongate in the Old Town of Edinburgh. The adoption of the Maltese Cross, which adorns this attractive mid-eighteenth century house as well, as their emblem was in consequence of their occupation for almost three hundred years of the island of Malta, an occupation brought to an end by Napoleon in 1798.

The Order of St. John was reorganised on a purely charitable basis in 1827 and is now probably best known for its management of the St. John Ambulance Association in England. In Scotland this ancient Order of Chivalry was revived in 1948 and, in addition to the former Hospice in Trinity, Hospices were established at Carberry and Glasgow, all providing short-stay accommodation for the infirm or convalescent elderly.

By the beginning of the twentieth century Leith Mount, Nos 28 and 30 Ferry Road, had become the manse of North Leith Church. A large villa with a gate, or gardener's, lodge, out-buildings and a stable, and its interior in need of modernisation, it appeared, to the members of the Edinburgh Town Council, to be an appropriate site for a new town hall and branch library for Leith. The provision of these facilities was seen as part of the City's obligation to the Port after the 1920 amalgamation, an obligation which was considered to be honourably discharged when the villa, which had been built about 1818, and its grounds were purchased in 1924 for £3600. A new manse for the church was acquired for £2000 at No 26 Lomond Road in Trinity and work started on what is now the Leith Theatre and the public library in 1929. At the extreme east end of the library facade is carved

> Leith Town Hall and Library.
> This stone was laid by The
> Right Hon. Sir Alexander
> Stevenson, LL.D., Lord
> Provost, 11th October 1929.

CHAPTER 4

Schools

THE innovators in Leith in the teaching of children appear to have been the canons of St. Anthony's Preceptory, a religious house founded by Sir Robert Logan of Lestalric, later Restalrig, in 1435, and dedicated by Henry Wardlaw, Bishop of St. Andrews, in the same year. It stood on the west side of St. Anthony's Lane at the Henderson Street end and the street known as Yardheads ran later behind the retaining wall of the Preceptory and the orchards for which it was well known. Although it is not clear exactly when the school commenced, it would be at a date subsequent to 1496 when the Scottish Parliament passed an Act which decreed that

> It is statute and ordained throw all the Realme that all Barrounes and Freeholders that ar of substance put their Eldest Sonnes and aires to the Schules fra they be six or nine years of age, and till remaine at the Grammar-schules quhill they be competentlie founded and have perfite Latine. And therefore to remaine at the Schules of Art and Jure so that they may have knowledge and understanding of Lawes etc. .... and what Barroune or Free-holder of susbstance that holdis not his sonne at the schules ... he sall pay to the King the summe of twenty pound.

The Grammar Schule would have been in existence for some time when, on the 20th of July 1521, the master is recorded to have 'allegit and said that hiddertills he was redy at all tymes after his power till resist aganis the Inglismen and the King's rebelles ... and protestit for remeid and help'. This declaration of militant loyalty to the Crown was made by the schoolmaster, however, not in his professional capacity but in his other position, under

48

the Bailie for South Leith, of chief deputy officer of the town's defences. It was only eight years since the terrible defeat of Flodden, and Scotland, then living in its long-lasting aftermath, required the bailies of Edinburgh to report from time to time on their state of preparedness for an English attack across the Border. Leith had no bailies of its own as the port was under the superiority of the capital city and remained in that condition until the passing, in 1833, of the Parliamentary Reform Act.

Grammar schools were so called because the principal subject taught in them was Latin grammar, a beneficial consequence being the pupils' exposure to the great works of literature written in that language — the language of the Church, the professions and the Acts of Parliament in the Middle Ages. To be ignorant of Latin was to be outside the pale of European culture and out of touch with contemporary European thinking, and for long the teacher of Latin was the only teacher in a school.

In order to meet the constant demand for young male voices for the choral services, 'Sang Schools', or 'Music Schools', were introduced for the training of boys, who had also to be able to read, sing and chant. Sometimes called the 'Reader's School' as it was taught by the reader or session clerk, it was also known as the 'vulgar school' because the children were only taught their own mother tongue and no pretensions were made to the higher education afforded by the Grammar School. Sang Schools later developed into parish schools and were quite inde-pendent of Grammar Schools which were the forerunners of the Burgh Schools.

The Reformation, which became absolute in Scotland in 1560, was responsible for important and far-reaching changes, some of which were not effected without turmoil and disorder. But the Reformed Church placed education high among its priorities. On the 10th of June 1572 the lands, buildings and revenues of St. Anthony's Preceptory were granted to the town of Leith by James VI who declared his wish that good rule should be preserved by 'upholding Schools for the education of children in literature within the said toun of Leith'. In 1596 the property and revenues were given to the Kirk Session of South Leith Church when that body immediately presented a memorial to the King for permission to impose a duty on imported wine for the 'susteyning of ane scole-masteris in the said toun and provision of their stiependis.' James consented and from then until the High School was opened on the Links in 1806 the educational authority in the port was the Kirk Session of South Leith Church who provided and maintained a grammar school for the affluent and, as the teaching of music was not prohibited after the Reformation, a music school for the poor for which, in 1613, the elders purchased a pair of double virginals. This school had been held in the Cantore, a little room in a building which stood in the Kirkgate at the entrance to South Leith churchyard. Shortly after the Reformation this was taken over for use as a prison and the scholars were accommodated in King James's Hospital which had been built in the south-west corner of the churchyard about 1614. In 1643 the Session decided that 'the reader should have the Convening House in ye hospital qlk appertains to ye maltmen, traffickers and crafters' to be a school till he got a house provided for him. No house was ever made available, however, and the school remained there until it was moved to Leith Links in 1806.

The Grammar School appears to have been held in Trinity House as in 1636 the Kirk Session permitted 'ye skipers to have ye keay of ye gramer scool qlk is ye Leith Ternitie house'. Later, in 1643, it was stated to be 'under ye almes house' which again is a reference to Trinity House in the Kirkgate. A few years afterwards Leith was occupied by Cromwell when the school was turned out and took refuge in a loft in Dubraw above the soap house, while the Trinity House vaults became an army store. It was allowed to return in 1657 and to remain in the 'laigh vout' of Trinity House until 1710 when it was transferred to the King James Hospital where the music school had been housed. It was visited by the Kirk Session either quarterly or halfyearly, as they themselves decided, but a visit was sometimes requested by the master himself when he wanted to show off 'ye children's proficiencie' and therefore his own teaching skill as well. School hours were from 6 am to 6 pm — a long time to spend in the vaults of Ternitie House or even in the loft above the soap house in Dubraw!

One of the results of the 1833 Reform Act was the vesting, in 1848, of the High School Trust in the Magistrates and Town Council of Leith. A High School Trust Committee of management was set up and this body operated until 1872 when all authority was transferred to the Leith School Board. The old High School of Leith was renamed Leith Academy in 1888 and the present Leith Academy Secondary School, with its crowning cupola, beside the Links in Duke Street was built in 1931.

The Minutes of Leith Town Council of 11th July 1840 record a request from the Committee of the Leith Gymnastic Games in which the petitioners 'pray that your Honourable Board will Grant them a small portion of the Links of Leith, and more especially that part before the High School', as the games were to be 'played off on Wednesday the 22nd July'. The Council agreed, with the concurrence of the Tenant of the Links (which were let at intervals of a few years to the highest bidder), but the petitioners were strictly prohibited from erecting any 'Booths or tents for the sale of drink or the vending of any spiritous or intoxicating Liquors on the Links'. No doubt the High School boys took part in the games, and some may also have been among the 'idle boys who chase the Horses up and down' the Links 'to the injury of the Gravel Walks and the great danger of the inhabitants', as a Councillor unable to be present at a Council meeting complained in a letter in 1839, the previous year. 'I beg

c

you will call attention to the manner in which the Tenant of the Links is acting in allowing so many Horses, Asses etc. to be turned out without any person seemingly to take charge of them. . . . I am sure the Council have no right to deprive the inhabitants of the privilege of walking, and their children playing, on the Links which have been granted them by Act of Parliament. I hope it will never again be let but for a sheep to go on, and in the meantime the Tenant ought to keep some person there.' The Clerk reported that he had sent for the Tacksman who had undertaken to remedy the nuisance.

The amenity of the Links was still a matter for debate in the old Council Chamber in February 1905 when 'it was resolved to take no further action in regard to the formation of a pond on the Links, the cost being regarded as prohibitive.' At the same time a 'recommendation by the Parks Committee regarding the removal of the wall of North Leith Public Park bounding Largo Place was approved. A new railing, similar to those on the Links, is to be erected, the walks and paths renewed, and a set of swings and a Maypole erected, all at a cost of £70.' The swings and the Maypole may perhaps have kept that generation of idle boys sufficiently entertained and therefore less likely to injure the gravel walks and endanger the inhabitants.

The district of Trinity itself, better known for the distinction of its Georgian and Victorian domestic architecture, is not often thought of as a home of education, but it made good provision for the scholastic instruction of its children. At the turn of the century Sir John Murray's two daughters from Challenger Lodge (now St. Columba's Hospice) were among the pupils at Miss Yule's School. This establishment was run by three prim, Victorian maiden ladies, Miss Yule herself, who was of course the eldest, Miss Frances and Miss Chrissie. It started in Trinity Villa in York Road, then moved to North End House at the north-west corner of Trinity Road and

Lennox Row, then to a former nunnery in Russell Place and was finally located in No 33 East Trinity Road. They employed a music teacher, a dancing mistress, a 'Mademoiselle' for French and the artist Miss Annie Morgan, who lived with her sister and their parents in Woodville in Laverockbank Road and who gave instruction in painting and drawing. After their retirement the two surviving sisters continued to live in their home in East Trinity Road (and were still alive at least up to the time of the Second World War) and the school was moved next door to No 31. The name was then changed to the Lixmount School for Girls and Boys and the new Principal was Miss S. Campbell. The Howard Academy, a preparatory school for boys and girls, was run by Miss Hutchings at No 4 Denham Green Place, and these two small schools continued to provide early educational facilities for Trinity children during the 1930s and '40s.

The recent redevelopment of the site of Denham Green House, which was donated by the Salvesens of Trinity to the Edinburgh Academy when it became the Junior Department of their Preparatory School, is referred to under *Houses in and near Trinity*.

Bonnington Academy (another private school also known as Hunter's Academy) was conducted in Catherine Bank, No 174 Newhaven Road, by the master, Mr Davidson Hunter, during the later decades of the nineteenth century and the first thirty years or so of the twentieth, by which time the master was James W. Hunter, MA. The building consists of two Georgian houses with their front doors very close together, No 174 being on the northern side, on the east side of the road.

On the north side of Ferry Road and facing Chancelot Terrace was Afton Lodge in which resided The Rev Dr John Hutchison, minister of Bonnington United Free Church. He had come to Bonnington from Renfrew in 1877 when the congregation was newly formed. In July 1926 he left on the yacht *Hersilia* to make a tour of Egypt

Trinity Academy, originally known as Craighall Road Public School, was opened in 1894.

and the Holy Land but took ill and died at Constantinople. His son, the advocate Mr, later Sir, George Aitken Clark Hutchison, was a member of Parliament for many years and was the father of Lieut.-Commander Sir George Ian Clark Hutchison, MP for West Edinburgh from 1941 - 59. Afton Lodge stood in four acres of ground, ample space for expansion when, in 1907, it became Holy Cross Academy, a training college for Roman Catholic teachers, for which purpose it was extensively altered. It was later demolished and the site, behind the old retaining wall, is now occupied by the Lothian Regional Council school, Holy Cross Primary.

Trinity Academy, originally known as Craighall Road Public School, was opened on the 3rd of February 1894

Flora Clift Stevenson, LL.D. (1839-1905). She performed the opening ceremony at Trinity Academy and died while Chairman of the Edinburgh School Board. (Photograph by courtesy of Edinburgh City Libraries).

by Miss Flora C. Stevenson (the present-day Lothian Regional Council school which bears her name is in Comely Bank). The school had been functioning for five months before its official opening ceremony and speeches of welcome to Miss Stevenson were made by several of the children. There were also exhibitions by the infant department and a series of performances by the senior division. One pupil said that not only was the school provided with all that was necessary for teaching them 'what was required for doing well the work of life, but also to acquire every useful accomplishment'. The secondary department gave education in the higher subjects of science and art and 'it would be their own fault if they did not take advantage of them'. They trusted that the Board would never regret providing 'this splendid building' and appreciated that Miss Stevenson, a member of the Edinburgh School Board, had done a great deal in the interests of education and that her coming to open their school was another proof of that interest.

While there is no doubt that few schoolchildren of the late twentieth century would be disposed to express such sentiments, it may even be suspected that those worthy pronouncements were written by the teachers rather than the pupils!

They were followed by a representative of the Leith School Board who said that, after their election in April 1888, almost the first thing they had to consider was a letter from the Scottish Education Department demanding that three thousand additional places be added to the school accommodation of the burgh. The plans of Couper Street School, a site for which had been acquired by the preceding Board, were immediately prepared and building proceeded with with all possible despatch. That school, which made provision for nineteen hundred pupils, had been opened in November 1890 and a suitable site for a school in the Trinity district, after a good deal of enquiry and negotiation, had been obtained in Craighall Road from General Clerk-Rattray (of the family who had acquired the lands of Bonnington in 1786 and whose Perthshire estate had given its name to Craighall Road) as early as October 1888 at a feuduty of £80 per acre. The extent of the ground was exactly one acre as the superior had declined to feu less.

Pending the completion of Couper Street School, the Board commenced building operations at Craighall Road, deciding that the school should provide fourteen hundred places and advertising for competitive plans. Twenty applications were received and Mr Barclay, the architect of the Govan School Board, was appointed the adjudicator. The first premium was awarded to the Leith architect, Mr George Craig, who had designed Lochend Road, Couper Street and several other schools for the Leith School Board. The Board's chairman laid the foundation stone at Craighall Avenue on the 11th of July 1891 and the school was finally completed in the summer of 1893. The accommodation for scholars was reduced to twelve hundred places as space was required for a science laboratory and lecture room and to meet the needs of cookery and laundry work as well as classrooms for music and sewing. The cost of the school, including furnishings, was about £18,000.

Between the date of planning and the date of completion of the school later to be known as Trinity Academy important measures affecting Scottish education had been passed by Parliament. Fees had hitherto been paid by their parents for every pupil in every public school in Scotland, but now elementary education up to sixth standard was, with certain exceptions, entirely free. There were two classes of school, those in the first class receiving the ordinary Parliamentary Grant but for which the managers did not claim a fee grant, and those in the second class being established with the sanction of the Scottish Education Department and receiving a fee grant of twelve shillings per scholar in addition to the ordinary Parliamentary grant and the school revenue. Another new measure was that under which the amount of £60,000 was allocated out of what was called the Equivalent Grant for secondary education in Scotland. Of that sum the share falling to Leith worked out at approximately one thousand pounds per annum. Many Leith parents at this time, anxious to obtain the best possible education for their sons and daughters, were sending them to fee-paying schools in Edinburgh with the result that over one thousand children resident in Leith were attending Edinburgh schools. It had therefore been agreed that, as a compromise, fees would be charged at Craighall Road School but the Secondary Department would be free. The number of pupils was 898 of which 705 were in the fee-paying department and 193 in the secondary, or free, department. A child entering at the age of five should be able to leave properly equipped for university entrance.

Flora Stevenson then addressed the assembled company and, on congratulating the Board on the beautiful building in which they were gathered, made particular reference to the many additional subjects which were now added to the school curriculum and which therefore made larger accommodation a pressing necessity. She also paid tribute to the educational advances in Leith during the past few years and made special mention of the secondary department as being a distinctive feature of the school.

After Miss Stevenson Mr W. Scougall, HM Inspector of Schools, addressed the children, who no doubt sat quietly and attentively through all the speech-making. He urged them to take the opportunity now being given to prepare themselves to become noble and useful men and women in after life and to be a school of which Leith could be justly proud.

Some interesting details about the school building are that it was heated by hot water pipes and ventilated by gas extractors in the roof, that the corridors were all fireproof and the walls lined with ornamental tiles, and that the rooms were "varnished pitch pine." Outside, on the top pediment on the principal facade on Craighall Avenue is a carved figure of youth bearing a torch of learning and, on the wall facing Craighall Road, a pedimented stone tablet commemorating the opening of the school. The building itself is of grey Hailes stone with all the dressings of red

Now St. Mary's Workshops, the former Yardheads School, originally built in 1876, still stands in Giles Street.

Dumfries stone. The janitor's lodge can still be seen in Craighall Road.

With an adjacent preparatory department opened later in Newhaven Road, these buildings carried the school through seven decades of the twentieth century. But, in spite of the extensions built in 1957 and 1962, accommodation was again creating problems by 1973 when, on the 18th of October, an Edinburgh newspaper, reflecting popular opinion, asked 'Is it fair that pupils and staff should be asked to face such intolerable conditions of overcrowding in Trinity Academy?' As the school leaving age had been raised and there had been some educational reorganisation in the city, extra classrooms were urgently required. The stage had been reached in which the children

Wardie Primary School, opened in 1931, lies on the west side of Trinity. Part of its extensive grounds was occupied by a Royal Navy Camp during the Second World War.

were being taught in the dining room, in the main hall which had had to be partitioned, in the corridors and even in the cloakrooms. The city architect was trying to speed up the immediate provision of temporary classroom units and an appeal was being made to Government for assistance in financing the provision of additional teaching space.

These difficulties having been overcome, and with an Annexe in North Junction Street which was formerly the David Kilpatrick School (also designed by George Craig and built in 1915), Trinity Academy, still occupying its original site and having a Parents' Association, one of the first in Britain, established in 1923, has gone on to serve the community at the present day as a lively and forward-looking school providing a sound education for the less inhibited successors, and probably in many cases the descendants, of those demure Victorian scholars who listened like models of submission and good behaviour to Flora Stevenson, less than a hundred years ago, at the formal official opening of the school.

George Craig, who designed so many of the schools in Leith, also carried out the reconstruction of Yardheads School in Giles Street in 1888. Built originally in 1876 for the Leith School Board, as stated on a plaque on the front elevation, the school is now, under the Scottish Development Agency, St. Mary's Workshops.

Over to the west, on the Trinity side of Granton Road, is Lothian Regional Council's Wardie Primary School laid out rectangularly around a central court. It was officially opened on the 15th of September 1931, many of the pupils (96 boys and 132 girls between the ages of five and twelve) having transferred from both Bonnington and Trinity Academies. By so doing 'they saved themselves', as their 1981 Jubilee Booklet (published by the Wardie Parents' Association) points out, 'the daily journey by steam train from Granton Road Station to Trinity Station'. The first Headmaster was Mr W. Myles.

In September 1939, on the outbreak of the Second World War, 403 of the 634 children were evacuated (though not for long) to Fife, while the school was occupied by ARP (Air Raid Precautions) personnel. By early 1940, however, most of the pupils had returned and, while classes were resumed in the school, the Royal Navy Camp known as HMS *Lochinvar* was built at the north end of the extensive playing fields which stretched down to Boswall Road. The school turned over some of its ground adjoining Netherby Road to be used as allotments where the children were allowed, under supervision, to 'dig for victory'. At the end of the War homeless persons of many nationalities were housed in Lochinvar Camp for a number of years.

But by far the most distinguished of these educational establishments was the school still known today, although in another and much more spacious environment, as Cargilfield. This famous boys' preparatory boarding school (the oldest preparatory school in Scotland) was founded in 1873 by The Rev Daniel Charles Darnell who lived in the now demolished West Darnell House, the schoolhouse being the former mansion of Cargilfield on the west side of South Trinity Road. Then part of Trinity Road, it followed the edges of long-vanished fields and thus took a winding course from Ferry Road at Goldenacre to Trinity Crescent, as the present Trinity Road still does.

Dr Darnell's grand-daughter, born in 1900 and now resident in Edinburgh, remembers being told about the early days and origins of the school. The founder had been a master at Rugby with very decided views on the education and upbringing of the young. Believing strongly in the benefits of fresh air and a situation near the sea, he came to Edinburgh for the purpose of establishing a school for boys which would fulfil both of these criteria. Being close to the fresh sea breezes of the Forth, he walked through Trinity in search of suitable premises for his project and decided initially in favour of one of the large houses in Primrose Bank Road. When he came to consider an appropriate name, however, second thoughts prevailed — Primrose Bank School was not one which would be calculated to appeal to boys! So it was to (South) Trinity Road that Dr Darnell now turned his steps and his attention, and found a habitation that met with his requirements — and to its name of Cargilfield he could see no possible objections.

The preparatory school, of which he was the first headmaster, quickly acquired a reputation for excellence to which Dr Darnell's emphasis on health may have been a contributory factor. He favoured open windows to provide continual fresh air within the building and gave his young pupils the opportunity to go swimming from the Chain

The last remaining entrance lane to the former 18th century villas in South Trinity Road now leads to Newbank Lodge. A similar drive once led to the house of Cargilfield of which there are no known views.

Pier as well as in the school's own swimming baths. Every Sunday they set out on the (uphill) walk to St. Paul's (now St. Paul's and St. George's) Episcopal Church in York Place which became their regular place of worship and gave the added bonus of a health-promoting walk in both directions.

After twenty-five years in Trinity the number of pupils wishing to attend had increased to the point where new and purpose-built accommodation was required. This was achieved in 1899 when the present premises at Barnton were completed, and at this time Dr Darnell decided to sell the school he had so successfully created and which had become a feeder school for Fettes College. Returning to England, he settled in Portsmouth as a clergyman and did not again re-enter the teaching profession. Partial reconstruction of the school at Barnton was carried out in 1962 and again in 1973. It is no longer exclusively for boys and had a female Head of School for the first time in 1990.

The situation of the old Cargilfield House was between the demolished Bellfield House, which lay immediately to the south of Cargil Terrace, and the two houses (also demolished) known as West Viewfield and East Viewfield below which, to the south, stood Rose Park, Newbank and, beyond the railway line, Trinity Cottage at Goldenacre. Long, narrow lanes, or paths, led to these houses from (South) Trinity Road (that to the former Rose Park being the only one still extant) and the present single-storey shop at No 23 between the tenement blocks was built across the entrance to Bellfield House. Cargil Court, with access from Cargil Terrace, has been laid out on the site of Bellfield and its garden where numerous apple trees once grew beside the house. And a dwellinghouse in South Trinity Road is said to have been built over the tiles of the swimming baths of Cargilfield School.

The school premises here were enlarged when East and West Viewfield were both taken over in addition to Cargilfield House and the last headmaster in the old buildings was Mr Harry Cotterill Tillard, MA, in 1899. Among the distinguished Old Boys of the school are Lord MacLeod of Fuinary (The Rev Dr George MacLeod, founder of the Iona Community (b. 1895)) and the Rt Hon George Younger, a former Secretary of State for Scotland and, subsequently, Secretary of State for Defence.

Cargil Terrace and Darnell Road take their respective names from the house in which the school was founded and its founder.

CHAPTER 5

Artists

IF Robert Gilfillan was the Poet of Leith, there are several contenders for the title of its Painter, one of them being Erskine Nicol, ARA, RSA (1825 - 1904). In the early months of 1925 the columns of the *Edinburgh and Leith Observer* contained repeated references to the approaching centenary of Nicol's birth on the 3rd of July 1825 which, together with his baptism, had been duly recorded in South Leith. The records, however, made no mention of an address. On the two-hundredth anniversary of the birth of John Home, the author of *Douglas*, an inscribed tablet had been placed on the house in Quality Street, (now Maritime Street) in Leith, where he had been born, and several people were of the opinion that a similar honour should be accorded to the man who had been held in such high regard, in England as well as in Scotland, as a Victorian artist. But where was the house, and was it still in existence in the port? No-one seemed to know and interest in the search for Erskine Nicol's birthplace was reflected in the space devoted to it in the *Observer*.

In April he was traced to No 6 Fife Place, a short street on the north side of Leith Walk just before Pilrig Church, and although no longer known by that name the buildings were still as they had been in Nicol's day. Had the house (or tenement flat) been found on which to place a suitable inscription? Unfortunately it had not. It was from this address that his first work - a still life - to be accepted by the Royal Scottish Academy had been sent when he was only sixteen years of age, but it did not necessarily follow that he had been born there.

Then, in May, came a letter from the artist's son, Mr J. Watson Nicol, written from Hampstead. He had been shown a copy of the *Observer* and would have been

The birthplace of John Home, the author of *Douglas*, in Maritime Street, as it appears today.

pleased to provide the required information had that been possible. His father, he said, had lived as a young boy in Lochend Road, but that house had long ago disappeared and he was not certain if that was in fact his place of birth. All he could confirm was that he must have lived in Fife Place after leaving Lochend Road. He did, however, have his self-portrait in water-colour painted in 1850.

It was therefore concluded that Erskine Nicol was probably born in Lochend Road but, the house being no longer there, the preparation of a commemorative plaque would have to be abandoned. In the edition of the *Observer* dated 4th July 1925, the day following the centenary of his birth, however, a long account is given of

Erskine Nicol, RSA. His paintings of Ireland and the Irish first brought this Leith artist to public attention. (Photograph by courtesy of The Royal Scottish Academy, Edinburgh).

both the painter and his work. 'This great artist', it reports, had exactly one hundred years ago been born in Leith and 'considering the fame he has achieved it is humiliating that his centenary has been to all intents and purposes ignored by his townsmen'. This is followed by a sketch of his 'notable career' which had ended at his death just twenty-one years before. The writer of this sketch was a regular contributor, on the history of the port, to the *Edinburgh and Leith Observer*, using the pseudonym of 'Restalrig'. His name was John Thomas Barclay Symons (1869–1928). Born at No 13 Tolbooth Wynd, he lived in his early years in a house in Charlotte Street which was entered from Charlotte Lane and, after spending some time in London writing music hall sketches, he settled finally in Glasgow. Later he became the sole partner of the Scottish National Press and his *Poems and Verses*, published in 1914, sold out in three days. A strong opponent of the amalgamation of Leith and Edinburgh, when that much lamented event took place in 1920 he founded the Port of Leith Association and was its first secretary. He died suddenly in May 1928.

Erskine Nicol was the son of James Main Nicol, an employee of Wauchope, Moodie & Hope, wine merchants, in Constitution Street. His artistic development and education were obtained at the Trustees' Academy in Edinburgh where he became a student, in spite of discouragement from his family, at the age of twelve. He had to make his living by teaching as well as painting and appears at one time to have been a drawing master in the old High School on the Links. After spending three or four years in Dublin he returned to Edinburgh in 1851 when his pictures, which were principally of Irish subjects, met with immediate success, many being sold almost before they were completed, and commissions were 'pouring in'. He lived for a year or two in Fettes Row, removing from No 13 to No 15, and when his studio was at the latter address, in 1856, he had no fewer than twenty paintings in the annual exhibition of the RSA of which he was elected an Associate in 1855 and a Royal Scottish Academician four years later.

Moving to London in 1861, he was made an Associate

Irish Emigrant landing at Liverpool by Erskine Nicol. (Photograph by courtesy of The National Gallery of Scotland).

of the Royal Academy in 1866 but the final accolade of Royal Academician was not bestowed. He was active at the same period as such prominent Scottish artists as

Sir W.Q. Orchardson and the brothers Faed and there were those who were persuaded that feelings ran strongly 'against Scotsmen at that time because there were so many outstanding artists' north of the border in competition with their English counterparts!

Erskine Nicol's work in his later years consisted largely of water-colour drawings, many of which were executed at Torduff House in Colinton where he lived for a short time, and numerous engravings of his work were also made. He was married twice and there were three children of each marriage. His death occurred on the 8th of March 1904 at Feltham, Middlesex, in his seventy-ninth year.

A posthumous exhibition of his work took place in the Bennett Gallery, Glasgow, in June 1915 when a price of about three hundred and fifty guineas was paid for many of the pictures. Such success, said a reviewer, was 'phenomenal when one considers that we are in the midst of the greatest war in the history of the world', but regrets were expressed that the exhibition had not been held in Leith.

Robert Gavin (1827 - 83) was also born in Leith and, although he lived and worked in Edinburgh, he travelled frequently abroad in search of subjects with which he felt in sympathy. In his early years Gavin painted the rustic Scottish countryside of landscape and village but was lured to America in 1868 to record on canvas the dark-skinned features of those who were linked by ancestral ties to the continent of Africa. And it was there, in Tangier, that he afterwards settled for several years, producing a series of Moorish pictures and finding inspiration for subsequent work on his return, his last visit to Africa being as late as 1880.

Elected an Associate of the Royal Scottish Academy in 1855, Robert Gavin attained the rank of Academician in 1879. Like many artists the Edinburgh addresses from which his works were sent for exhibition at the Academy were subject to frequent change. From 1846 to 1852 he lived in James's Place, Leith Links, first at No 11 and then at No 12. The following year he removed to 15 Gayfield Square and, four years later, to No 34. In 1859 his address is given as '25 Haddington Place, Edinburgh' (probably, along with 10 North St. Andrew Street a year later, a studio only), 'and 2 Laverock Bank, Trinity', and from there he went, in 1863, first to 38 Dublin Street and then to 25 Sheriff Brae in Leith, followed by 11 Bonnington Place, Trinity, and Shelbourne Bank, Newhaven Road. After staying briefly at No 1 London Street and, for about eight years, at 15 Brandon Street, his final removal was to Cherry Bank, Newhaven Road, where his death took place on 5th October 1883, at the age of fifty-five.

He painted principally portraits and genre subjects, his Diploma Work in the RSA collection being *The Moorish Maiden's First Love*. He also painted the portrait of The Rev Dr Stevenson of South Leith Church. The Academy, at a Council meeting held on 12th October, announced the death 'of their brother Academician, Robert Gavin, who has long held an honourable place on the roll of Scottish painters'. His African pictures had 'added greatly to his reputation, and their absence from the walls of the Academy will be a loss of much that was interesting in the Annual Exhibitions'.

Truly an undoubted son of Leith, as not only was he born and educated (at the High School) there but died not far away in Brunswick Street, was John Smart, RSA, RSW (1838 - 99). His career in art began when he was apprenticed to his father, an engraver, and he also attended the Board of Trustees School of Design, taking several prizes, from 1853 to 1858. Having for a short time studied landscape painting under Horatio MacCulloch, John Smart exhibited his first picture at the Royal Scottish Academy in 1860, contributing regularly to the Annual Exhibitions for the rest of his life.

The scenery of Wales and the Lowlands of Scotland attracted him for a time, but it was the grandeur and beauty of the Highlands, and the simple, crofting life of its people, to which, almost exclusively, he devoted his talents in succeeding years. Elected an Associate of the Academy in 1871, he attained the status of Academician five years later, his Diploma Work in the RSA collection being *Far from the Busy World*.

John Smart's first painting to be exhibited at the Academy was submitted from No 20 Elm Row, at the top of Leith Walk, in 1860, but the four pictures sent the following year (*Highland Lake: Rain Clearing Off, Sketch in the Highlands, Old Churchyard, Roslin* and *Study of an Elm Tree, near Kelso*) were from No 9 Smith's Place, further down Leith Walk. In 1863 his address was 16 Picardy Place where he remained until 1873 when he removed to No 4. From 1885, and for the rest of his life, he lived at 13 Brunswick Street, Hillside, and it was here that his death occurred on the first of June 1899.

This noted landscape artist was also an accomplished water-colour painter and among his pictures in that medium was a series entitled *The Golfing Greens of Scotland* which were subsequently etched by George Aikman, ARSA.

George Ogilvie Reid (1851 - 1928) was born in Leith and began his career as an engraver. He started painting, however, in both oil and water-colour at an early age and in a wide variety of subjects which included landscape, portraiture and Jacobite history. In 1891 he was commissioned by Queen Victoria to depict the baptismal service of the Prince of Battenberg at Balmoral and the studies which he made at that time were bequeathed by him to the Royal Scottish Academy. His painting, lent by Her Majesty the Queen, *First Baptism for 300 years of a Royal Prince in Scotland, Balmoral Castle, October 31, 1891* was hung on the Academy's walls during the 1893 Exhibition, and another, also painted in 1891, entitled *The First Baptism of a Royal Prince in Scotland since 1591. Study of*

Picture submitted to Queen Victoria, was exhibited in 1914.

Ogilvie Reid became an Associate of the Royal Scottish Academy in 1888 and an Academician ten years later, his Diploma Work, one of his numerous Jacobite paintings, being *After Killiecrankie*. Over a prolonged period he visited Killin in Perthshire, for which he had a great affection, each summer and many of his landscapes painted in the surrounding countryside were regular features of the Academy's exhibitions. In London a favoured position on their walls was always accorded to him by the Royal Academy where he was held in high regard.

From 1884 to 1891 he lived at No 20 George Street. Removing from there to Shandwick Place, he lived first at No 15 and, from 1899, at No 54. From 1908 the artist's pictures were submitted to the Academy from 41 Synod Hall, Edinburgh, and from 1921 from 11 Carlton Street.

G.O. Reid died on 11th April 1928 when the RSA recorded that a unique figure had 'passed away from Scottish Art, and his place in the ranks of the Academy can never be filled'.

The son of a Perthshire farmer, and born at No 7 Crown Street, Leith, John Duncan Fergusson, RBA (1874 - 1961) had no formal training as a painter and no initial intention of pursuing art as a career. In 1886 he was enrolled as a pupil in the Royal High School, the family home being at No 77 Ferry Road, and afterwards became a medical student with the ultimate aim of being accepted as a naval surgeon. This idea was abandoned, however, and, about 1894, Fergusson rented a studio in Edinburgh and began to sketch. Drawn to Paris a few years later and coming under the influence of Picasso, he settled there in 1905 where boats and shipping, for which he developed a particular fascination, were soon established as his principal subjects. This led naturally to his important work during the First World War when he was appointed to the War Artists Commission by the Admiralty.

J. D. Fergusson, the Leith-born artist who rose to world fame in the early years of the 20th century with such paintings as *The Blue Hat* now in the Edinburgh City Art Centre. (Photograph by Yevonde, courtesy of the Margaret Morris Movement).

Returning to Paris between the wars, his reputation rose as a member of the group of Colourists which included such famous names as Caddell and Peploe, though his own style remained distinct and individual. From 1940 he resided in Glasgow, where he founded the New Art Club and New Scottish Group, and he died there, at No 4 Clouston Street, on 30th January 1961.

J.D. Fergusson was married to Margaret Morris, the costume designer and exponent of modern dance who was the founder of the Margaret Morris Movement (the Movement is still in existence) summer schools in the early twentieth century and who died, at the age of eighty-eight, in 1980. One of Fergusson's best-known pictures, *The Blue Hat*, painted in 1909, is in the possession of the City of Edinburgh Art Centre.

An artist whose work is now receiving recognition after many decades of neglect is the great Scottish landscape painter, Horatio MacCulloch (1805 - 67). The son of a Glasgow weaver who styled himself a manufacturer, he was born in the second city and called after the hero of Trafalgar, Admiral Horatio Nelson, as he was born in the year of the great sea battle. In the latter part of his life, however, he lived, and died, in Trinity.

After serving his apprenticeship with a house painter, MacCulloch exhibited in Glasgow and in 1829 had his first picture hung at the Royal Scottish Academy of which he became an Associate in 1834. Four years later he achieved the status of Academician, and exhibited at the Royal Academy in London (of which he was never made an Academician) in 1843 where his pictures were not hung to his satisfaction. As a consequence he sent no further works to the Royal Academy. His subjects were exclusively Scottish and it has been claimed that he stood in the same relation to landscape painting in Scotland as Raeburn did to portraiture and Wilkie to domestic art and that he 'made nature his studio' by planting his easel in the open air. Shortly after becoming a Royal Scottish Academician

The great Scottish landscape painter Horatio MacCulloch who spent
the closing years of his life in Trinity. (Photograph by courtesy of
The Royal Scottish Academy, Edinburgh).

he removed to Edinburgh where he lived first at No 12
Howard Place, in Inverleith, and then in a house in
Danube Street in Stockbridge.

During the last years of his life Horatio MacCulloch
stayed in one of the Trinity Villas adjoining Trinity Grove,
a house which is still extant in Trinity Road although no
longer known by its old name. It was here in Trinity
Grove that John Ballantyne, the flamboyant but consump-
tive brother of James, the publisher of Sir Walter Scott,
lived, for about six years, till 1821. Hay Lodge, however, also has the reputation of being MacCulloch's home

in Trinity. It was the successor, on the same site, to the farmhouse of Trinity Mains which was built by the Masters and Mariners of Trinity House of Leith when they set up their farm on the Wardie Muir in 1713. The artist died in June 1867 and was buried at Warriston Cemetery where a monument, designed by James Drummond, RSA, in the form of a Celtic Cross, was erected to his memory. The cross is decorated on one side of the base with a palette and brushes and a laurel wreath and, on the other, with a bas-relief of his favourite dogs.

Leith, the thriving, bustling seaport with cargoes from every airt unloaded regularly at its quays, drew artists, like a magnet, to its harbour in the great days of sail. Alexander Naysmith (1758-1840) painted *The Port of Leith* (which hangs in the Edinburgh City Chambers), the old 'sheet' sails of the ships uplifted above the water, in 1824; P.J. Clays (1819-1900) gave the same title to a spirited, windswept canvas showing vessels tossing in a brisk sea breeze while Arthur's Seat rises darkly to landward and, in the foreground, men labour to control an open rowing boat on the crest of a wave; and William Fleming Vallance (1827-1904), a painter of the sea and shipping, depicted the splendid harbour scenes which were then a daily and familiar sight to the people of the port, many of whom had had the sea in their blood for generations.

The history of the burgh inspired such subjects as the landing of Mary Queen of Scots in 1561 which was portrayed, long after the event, by Sir William Allan (1782 - 1850) and other artists, and the famous arrival at the Shore of King George IV (at twenty minutes past noon) on the fifteenth day of August 1822. The crowded scene was painted by William Horne Lizars (1783 - 1859) and by Alexander Carse (whose date of birth is unknown but who is believed to have died in 1838). This observant artist, whose pictures show a wealth of detail and the gift of capturing the momentary humour in a situation, is less highly acclaimed than his contemporaries as he had little early training in his art. But his huge canvas (63in x 142.5in), which covers almost an entire wall in the old Council Chamber in Queen Charlotte Street, is full of interest. It shows the king, surrounded by a cheering, waving multitude of Edinburgh citizens, shaking hands with Bailie John McFie, the senior magistrate (Leith had no provost till 1833), and among the many minute ongoings in the crowd is a pickpocket at work, with his taking ways, amid the throng. One looks in vain, however, in this painting for Sir Walter Scott. A coloured engraving on paper after Carse with the title *Provost [sic] Macfie welcoming King George IV at Leith 1822*, by Robert Scott (1771 - 1841), can be seen in Huntly House Museum and another copy is in the Master's Room at Trinity House.

Carse exhibited at the first Edinburgh Exhibition in 1808 and also, frequently, at the Royal Academy in London in which city he lived for the last twenty-five years of his life.

CHAPTER 6

Museums

IN 1983 the Leith Museum Trust was set up with the
aim of preserving the rich and varied heritage of the
ancient port and several temporary exhibitions have been
held in recent years in Leith Library, the Customs House
and Lamb's House (the latter having once been considered as a possible location for the museum). Difficulties have, however, been encountered in obtaining a
suitable building in which to put artefacts and items of
interest on permanent public display. But Leith has had
its own museums in the past, and the first appears to
have been established in the Old Council Chamber by
the Leith Town Council on a date which must have been
subsequent to 1899 as, in a letter dated May 1899, a
correspondent in the *Leith Observer* enquired 'why not a
Leith museum?'

On the death of The Rev Walter M. Goalen, the rector
of Christ Church in Trinity Road, the Council had purchased, in 1890, his house and grounds of Starbank.
These gardens were some years later added to those of
the former Laverockbank House to form Starbank Public
Park, and the Council Chamber exhibits were transferred
in 1920 (after amalgamation with Edinburgh) to Starbank
House which remained the museum of Leith until 1932,
the contents then being taken to the museum established in
that year in Huntly House in the Canongate, although
some items which had been on loan were returned to their
owners at this time. The Canongate Tolbooth, opposite
Huntly House, became a museum in 1954 when what
remained of the Starbank Collection was moved to the
Tolbooth, the apartment in which it was exhibited being
known thereafter as the Leith Room. When this area was

The floral star and crescents on the seaward-facing slope of Starbank Park.

later required for other purposes the collection was again taken over by Huntly House.

Two of the items listed in the Starbank Collection related to Trinity itself - an ancient 'strike-a-light' found in Laverockbank Road and a Tax Notice of Assessment for 1815 (the year of Waterloo) which had been sent to Robert Menzies, Esq, at Lixmount, the house, now demolished, which with its grounds lay on the south side of East Trinity Road and was built in 1794. Here also are the keys of Bonnington Toll House which was pulled down in 1896 during operations carried out by the Caledonian Railway Company, two stamps of the Burgh of Leith, a £2 banknote dated 2nd March 1818 issued by the Leith Banking Company, a £1 note of the same bank dated 1838 and a copy of the 'Herald and Reformer and General Advertiser' of Saturday, 9th February 1876 printed and published by Charles Drummond of No 132 Kirkgate.

There are items of much greater antiquity such as the Grant by Robert Logan of Restalrig, knight, to his servitors and craftsmen of the 'Tailyour Craft' in Leith of

that power to form a fraternity and make statutes for the
same, 20 June 1515, the seal of the Burgh of Leith
date-stamped 1563, a Queen Elizabeth sixpence dated 1573
dug up in South Leith churchyard and a wooden panel
dated 1659 taken from the pew of the Tailors' incorporation in South Leith Church. A cannonball discovered
in Henderson Gardens in 1900 and thought to have
been fired from Mount Somerset (better known today as
Giant's Brae)* on Leith Links during the Siege of Leith in
1560 is also here. Amongst the books in the collection are the poem 'Peter McCraw' by Robert Gilfillan
(the 'Poet of Leith') and the orderly book of the Leith
Gentlemen Riflemen from 6th January to 15th November
1820. Another donation to the museum was an old dagger
found by excavating workmen at the construction of the
Imperial Dock, as were a woodcut block showing the
landing at the Shore of George IV in 1822, a medal
commemorating the same event and a knocker from the
door of the old Poorhouse in Great Junction Street. A
surprising survival are the ribbons from the torch with
which Provost Smith's wife lit the Leith Links bonfire on
the coronation day of George V on 22nd June 1911, and, a
more predictable one, pieces of shell which had been
dropped in Sandport Street by a' German Zeppelin on the
evening of Sunday the 2nd of April 1916.

The photographs in the collection include one taken
at the Edinburgh and Leith Corporations Gas Commissioners' ceremony at the formal opening of the second
section of Granton Gas Works by Lady Cranston and Mrs
Mackie (the wives of the respective provosts) on 15th
October 1906. There are communion tokens as well and a
number of weights and measures, one of which would no
doubt bring back vivid memories to those who did the
family shopping before the Second World War - a for-
pit weight of 1¾ lbs (which always seemed to be used,

* A map of 1560 recently acquired by the Leith Museum Trust shows
that there were no gun emplacements on Leith Links, thus disproving
an old Leith tradition.

Trinity House of Leith in the Kirkgate. The vaults which served as a schoolhouse for Leith children in the 17th century are still here and it was the Masters and Mariners of Trinity House who gave its name to Trinity by setting up their farm of Trinity Mains on the Wardie Muir. The house now contains an outstanding collection of nautical and Leith memorabilia.

in those distant days, exclusively for the purchase of potatoes!).

Opposite the Parish Church in the Kirkgate, its forecourt a garden with railings and a garden gate, stands Trinity House of Leith, continuing to the present day the long history and ancient traditions of the Fraternity of Masters and Mariners of the Port since its foundation in c 1380. Today the contents of Trinity House constitute a museum of nautical memorabilia of national importance and outstanding interest. Its roots lie deep in the charitable spirit that prevailed among the seafarers of the burgh who, as John Mason in his *History of Trinity House*, has written, 'imposed a levy of twelve pennies Scots on every ton of merchandise loaded or unloaded by Scottish ships at the port of Leith for the relief of the poor, the aged and the infirm of their calling'. It was known as prime gilt and in 1566 Mary Queen of Scots and Darnley ratified both the prime gilt and the institution of the Hospital, although the charter is no longer in existence. Their hospital, or almshouse, was built in 1555. The funds were later augmented by Crown Money, the masters and mariners deducting for each voyage made 'of ilk crowne two pennies', or its equivalent in foreign currency, to be placed in one of two boxes kept on each side of the 'brig of Leith'. These two sources provided the total income of the Fraternity but there were many irregularities, and rules were made to 'poynd the sails and anchors' of those shipmasters who refused to pay.

In the mid-seventeenth century Cromwell's troops took possession of the Hospital's lands and buildings and, turning out the school-children from the vaults of 'Ternitie House', converted them to an army, or commissary, store. Breaking open the charter chest, General George Monk (a letter in his handwriting is preserved in the House) had the Incorporation's documents taken to Stirling Castle and they were not returned until 1654. It was probably at this time that the Mary and Darnley charter disappeared. (The remaining records have been deposited in the Register House in Edinburgh where they can still be read). The Kirk Session of South Leith took the precaution of burying its charter chest and communion plate beneath the church floor where they lay undetected till the danger was past.

By the middle of the nineteenth century the 1555 building had, despite restoration in 1668 and subsequent repairs, fallen into decrepitude, and in 1816 it was replaced on the same site by the present House designed by the architect Thomas Brown. It cost £2500. The historic vaults,

D

however, have survived, and can still be entered from the courtyard at the back, as have two carved stones which are built into the exterior walls of the later building. One of them with an anchor and two triangles in relief and the date 1570, records (from Psalm 107, verses 23 and 24):

> They that goe down to the sea in shippes
> That doe business in the great Waters
> These see the works of the Lord
> And his wonders in the deep.

And on the other is carved:

> In the name of the
> Lord ye Masteris
> and Mareners bylis
> this Hous to ye pour
> Anno Domini 1555

Trinity House as rebuilt in 1816 is a classical conception of central two-storey block with single-storey flanking wings, the main facade and the projecting portico ornamented respectively with pairs of Ionic and Doric columns. Inside, in the Georgian-featured entrance hall, is a rare collection of old maps, the ancient iron-bound charter chest with three locks, and a veneered wooden ballot-box with the interior divided into two compartments and with a round, open projection for the insertion of the voter's hand. Among the wealth of historical material in the Master's Room are a print of James IV's famous warship *The Great Michael*, a framed map of Trinity dated 1838 showing Trinity Mains and, a most interesting item, a plan of the Suez Canal bearing portraits of the Khedive of Egypt and the great French engineer Ferdinand de Lesseps who was responsible for the Canal's construction and who has written in French his confirmation that the first passage of the waterway, before its official opening in

1869, was made by the S.S. *Danube* of Leith on its way to India. Laden with cotton, she also returned through the Canal in January 1870. A fortunate and interesting survivor, rescued from the previous building, is the fireplace in the Master's Room; it is made of black marble and cast iron and is decorated with nautical and other emblems. The two black marble fireplaces in the Convening Room are contemporary with the present building.

The first floor is reached by a splendid Imperial staircase lit by a First World War memorial stained glass window inserted in 1933. The large and impressive Convening Room occupies the whole of the upper storey, its west wall dominated by the huge canvas of Vasco da Gama rounding the Cape of Good Hope in 1497 by David Scott, RSA, which was acquired in 1849. Of the four Raeburn portraits in this room the most interesting is the fine painting of Admiral Duncan, who was given, among many other honours, the Freedom of the Incorporation, for which he returned a letter of thanks to Trinity House, after his victory at Camperdown in 1797. Raeburn was commissioned to paint his portrait for the House in the following year.

Elaborately framed and high on the wall is a small painting believed to be a portrait of Mary of Guise, the second wife of James V and the mother of Mary Queen of Scots, and among the many models of ships from the days of sail and of more recent times is the replica of a vessel which was once thought to be that in which Mary of Guise was borne to Leith. The monogram of King Christian IV of Denmark (reigned 1588 - 1648) has now been discovered on the taffrail of the model and, having therefore been a galleon of his Danish Navy, it may perhaps have brought another and later Queen, Anne of Denmark, the wife of Mary's grandson King James VI, to Scotland. The model dates from the opening years of the seventeenth century and is now in too frail a condition to be moved. It was consequently with regret that a recent request for its transport to Denmark for an exhibition there had to be declined.

The Leith provosts' chain of office (dated AD 1901) is among the many reminders of the past history of the burgh in the Convening Room. Having been bought by Provost Mackie, it was presented by him to the Leith Dock Commission on the demise of the Leith Town Council. It was then used by the Chairman of the Dock Commission until that body, which had been set up in 1826, was superseded by the Forth Ports Authority about thirty years ago. The chain's pendant, however, was replaced by a new one bearing the name of the Dock Commission and what became of the original is not now known. One of the smaller items is the china bowl, probably a punch bowl, which is an example of those which were once presented each year to the master of the first ship to enter the Baltic after the ice had broken.

The set of three dozen ladderback chairs in the style of Chippendale was ordered for the 1816 building. Made in the Canongate of Edinburgh, it cost exactly £36!

The ceiling of the Convening Room was renewed, for an additional fifty pounds, a year after the completion of the house as the original was not considered satisfactory. The present pink and blue ornamental plasterwork was then carried out incorporating dolphins, sailing ships and other maritime motifs.

At the ordination in 1865 of The Rev James Deans, the colleague and successor of The Rev Francis Muir of Junction 'Road' Church, a dinner, at which nearly a hundred people were present, was held in the Convening Room at Trinity House. During the course of his speech Mr Muir referred to the great picture of the 'Cape of Storms' which hung before him as he spoke. A presentation of plate was made to Mr Muir, while Mr Deans received a pulpit gown, a Psalm Book and a Bible.

This ancient institution has survived the waves and storms of six centuries of the turbulent history of Leith and has gathered into its care a museum collection rich in nostalgic recollection of those who have gone down to the sea in ships and those who have lived and laboured in the Port. It seems wholly appropriate that when George IV landed at the Shore in 1822 Trinity House, its members having presented a loyal address to 'the King's most Excellent Majesty', should have been illuminated, when the pageantry had passed, on that much-remembered August night.

CHAPTER 7

Monuments and Memorable Events

ROSEBANK Cemetery, entered now only by the gate in Pilrig Street, was laid out in 1846 in the grounds of the former Rosebank House, the home of Lord Reay in the mid-eighteenth century. In the north-west corner stands the tall, white Celtic Cross which commemorates one of the worst misfortunes sustained by the Leith community during the First World War - the Gretna train disaster.

At 3.45 am on Saturday, the 22nd of May 1915 a troop train carrying the Leith Battalion of the Royal Scots Territorials left Larbert, where they had been in training, for their intended eventual destination at the Dardanelles on what would have been their first experience of active service. Lt Col W. Carmichael Peebles was in command of the battalion which had been recruited in Leith, Portobello and Musselburgh - the Leith district of burghs. Ten miles north of Carlisle, at Quintinshill siding near Gretna, at a quarter to seven, when most of the men were still asleep, the troop train crashed into a local train on which there were few casualties as it was practically empty. Shortly afterwards the midnight express from Euston to Glasgow came round a curve and ploughed into the wreckage, greatly increasing the loss of life and injury already suffered by the battalion, and a fire, which persisted till the evening, was soon raging among the carriages and hindering the work of rescue which had begun at once. Col Peebles was unhurt and joined in the frantic attempts to release the injured which continued throughout the day, 'under a broiling sun' as one account described it, while firemen played water on the wreckage during the whole rescue operation.

Special trains were brought up, as well as ambulances and private cars, to convey survivors to the Cumberland

The headquarters of the Leith Battalion of the Royal Scots which served as a mortuary for the Gretna railway disaster victims.

Hospital in Carlisle. But it was soon filled to capacity, and hotels, schools and even some private houses were pressed into service as emergency accommodation. The few who were fortunate in escaping injury were given quarters in the barracks at Carlisle. As the day wore on, however, and the terrible toll of life was counted, out of 485 officers and men, 214 had been killed and of the others only about sixty were able, unaided, to answer a roll-call.

As news filtered through to Leith, relatives hurried to the Battalion Headquarters in Dalmeny Street, but definite information was slow in coming and telegrams of enquiry 'poured in all day' at the scene of the tragedy which had been caused, it was later established, by a signalman's error. (Three railway employees were subsequently committed for trial accused of gross negligence, at Carlisle Assizes). Lists of names were being posted on the wall of the Drill Hall at Dalmeny Street till well into the small hours of Sunday morning.

Later that day the bodies of over one hundred dead were brought to Leith Central Station and from there, watched by thousands of spectators, to the Drill Hall which became 'a huge mortuary', while the whole town went into mourning.

Some families arranged private burials in Warriston Cemetery, in the Eastern Cemetery in Easter Road and in Seafield and Piershill Cemeteries, but the principal and public interment took place in Rosebank on the Monday afternoon. The Rev James Harvey, minister of Lady Glenorchy's United Free Church, and The Rev William Swan, minister of South Leith Church, the Honorary Chaplains to the Battalion, conducted the main service in the Drill Hall, after which one hundred and one coffins were carried from the Hall and conveyed from Dalmeny Street to Rosebank where they were laid in one common grave in the north-west corner of the cemetery. The streets between the Drill Hall and Rosebank were lined with silent crowds and the solemn procession and burial ceremony lasted for three hours. Among those present were Sir J. Spencer Ewart, General Officer Commanding in Scotland, Lord Provost Inches of Edinburgh, Provost Malcolm Smith of Leith, Sir Richard Mackie, ex-Provost of Leith, and Col J. T. Salvesen (Lieut C. R. Salvesen was among the dead).

On Tuesday evening another twenty victims were brought to Leith and a second common grave was dug and a second public funeral held at Rosebank Cemetery.

It was agreed that a memorial should be erected to the memory of these young sons of Leith who had given their lives, as many of them would undoubtedly have done on the field of battle, in their country's service and an appeal was made for the sum of two thousand pounds, £1500 to

The Gretna Memorial in Rosebank Cemetery. The names of the 214 victims of the famous First World War train disaster are inscribed on the two sets of wall panels behind the Celtic Cross. (Photograph by Hamish Coghill).

endow a bed in Leith Hospital and £500 for a suitable monument.

Col Peebles had 'proceeded abroad with the other half of the Regiment' and on a brief visit to Edinburgh in April 1916 he was invited to a luncheon in the Leith

Council Chamber as an expression of 'the gratitude of Leith to him and the Battalion' who had played 'a glorious part in the warfare at Gallipoli'. Provost Smith proposed the health of Col Peebles whose brother had been killed when taking part in a 'great charge upon the Turkish trenches'.

By that time nearly four thousand pounds had been subscribed to the Gretna Memorial and it was decided that a donation should also be made to the Royal Scots Association as well as 'some substantial recognition to those institutions in the vicinity of Gretna which treated the victims of the disaster'. The monument, similar in style to St. Martin's Cross on Iona, was designed by George Simpson, the Burgh Architect, with panels containing the Leith Coat of Arms, the 7th Battalion crest and the Scottish Lion. On ten bronze panels on the wall behind were inscribed the names, in alphabetical order, of those who had died. All the sculptural work was carried out, in Peterhead granite, by John S. Rhind.

At three o'clock on the afternoon of Friday, the 12th of May 1916, the service of dedication commenced at Rosebank Cemetery where almost two thousand persons, including the subscribers to the monument and the victims' families, were assembled. A light rain was falling but did not deter the crowds who filled the streets outside. Both Chaplains, along with The Very Rev Dr A. Wallace Williamson, Dean of the Chapel Royal, conducted the service and the praise was led by a military band and a united choir of over a hundred voices. The Provosts of Edinburgh and Leith were joined by Sir John Spencer Ewart and Col Peebles, and the Earl of Rosebery, the Honorary Colonel of the Battalion, unveiled the Memorial. But the most poignant sight that day must surely have been the thirty survivors of the disaster, many of them supported by sticks and crutches, who were able to attend the final ceremony in honour of their fallen comrades. The wreaths and flowers that covered the ground in front of

The unveiling ceremony of the ornamental fountain in Starbank Park in 1910. It was donated by Mr. Thomas L. Devlin who stands on the left of the fountain. Mrs Devlin, who turned on the water supply, is in the middle holding a bouquet. (Photograph by courtesy of Mrs Angela Bertram).

the panels and around the Cross itself have gone, but the inscription on the front of the Cross still starkly records the tragic event and the stunned reaction to it:

> In memory of officers, non-commissioned
> officers and men 1:7th Battalion, The Royal
> Scots, Leith Territorial Battalion, who
> met their death at Gretna on 22nd May 1915
> in a terrible railway disaster on their
> way to fight for their country. This
> memorial and a bed in Leith Hospital
> are dedicated by mourning comrades and friends.

A sentence in the *Leith Observer* of the 29th of May of the previous year may well have been echoed by those present in Rosebank Cemetery that afternoon - 'It will be many a long day before the scene that was witnessed in the green meadow at Quintinshill on Saturday will be forgotten'.

Statue of King Edward VII (reigned 1901-10) in the robes of the Order of the Thistle in Victoria Park.

A service of commemoration was held annually in South Leith Church for a number of years.

Also in Rosebank is the grave of Queen Victoria's 'dresser', Ida Bouonomi, who died suddenly in 1852 while the Queen was in residence at Holyrood Palace.

An ornamental fountain, overlooking the sea, stands in the lower section of Starbank Park in Trinity. It was presented, as the inscription states, 'by Thomas L. Devlin, Esq, JP, Merchant, Newhaven' in 1910. Thomas Devlin was a fish salesman and steam fishing vessel owner operating from Granton, Newhaven, Glasgow and Aberdeen who lived, in the 1890s, at No 6 Annfield near the outflow to the Firth of the Anchorfield Burn. He had

Also in Victoria Park is this small fountain presented to the Burgh of Leith by the Leith Horticultural, Industrial and Sports Society in 1899.

started with a single vessel and had built up over the years a large fleet of trawlers.

Mr Devlin in fact donated two fountains, the other, much less elaborate than that at Starbank, being at the scene of his early home - 'a triangular piece of ground at Annfield'. (The Annfield fountain, however, is no longer there.) The same inscription was placed on both fountains and they were both opened on the same day in the May of 1910. From Annfield the assembled company journeyed to Starbank for the second ceremony by special tramcar. The water was turned on by Mrs Devlin who was then presented with a bouquet, after which cake and wine were

A large crowd watches the unveiling of the statue of Queen Victoria at the foot of Leith Walk in 1907. (Photograph by courtesy of Edinburgh City Libraries).

served in Starbank House which was by then in the ownership of the Town Council. As a mark of appreciation for his generosity, a silver salver was presented to Mr Devlin who took advantage of the occasion to make a further public-spirited gesture. The death of Edward VII had just taken place and, in the course of a short speech, he proposed that plans should be made for the erection at a suitable site of a memorial statue to the late King, immediately opening the fund himself with a donation of one hundred guineas. Provost Smith replied that he would gladly take the matter further and that he fully agreed with the proposal.

In the early years of the present century Thomas Devlin lived at Eversley, No 25 Stanley Road. He died in 1919.

The statue to Edward VII, who is represented in bronze wearing the robes of the Order of the Thistle, stands, facing Newhaven Road, in Victoria Park and was placed there three years later in 1913. John Stevenson Rhind (1859 - 1937) was the chosen sculptor for this memorial as well.

One of the military monuments in South Leith Churchyard is to the memory of Lieut Col Adam White, the fifth son of Adam White, the first Provost of the burgh who was an elder in South Leith Church for fifty years and who lived to the age of eighty-three. Adam, his son, joined the Indian Army, in which he served for twelve years, before he was twenty and, during a voyage home in 1822, spent the time writing *Considerations of the State of British India*. He became managing Governor of Upper Assam in 1835 and died, aged forty-eight, repelling a night attack by tribesmen on the 28th of January 1839.

In April 1901 a public meeting, at which there was 'a good attendance of influential gentlemen', was held in the Queen's Hotel in Leith for the purpose of commemorating 'the glorious reign of her late Majesty Queen Victoria'. The erection of a statue had been proposed and it was now decided to accept the Council's offer of 'a space at the foot of the Walk'. A fund-raising committee, consisting of Provost Mackie, who had called the meeting, and the Magistrates and Town Councillors, was then appointed and it was also unanimously agreed 'to form a Ladies' committee to assist in carrying through the project'. Their task accomplished, the sculptor of the Gretna Memorial, John S. Rhind, was commissioned to design the bronze statue of the Queen which was unveiled with pomp and ceremony in 1907 and which still stands, defying the late twentieth century traffic with imperial gaze, at the Foot of the Walk and, indeed, in front of the former Queen's Hotel, part of which has degenerated in recent years into a branch of Woolworth's Stores. The monument has, in fact, been moved several times, but never more than a few yards from its original position. Rhind was also responsible for the two panels which were added, on the pedestal, six years later. In one the Queen and Prince Albert are depicted arriving in Leith in 1842, while in the other volunteers are shown leaving their native shores to take part in the Boer War in South Africa.

Though not a burgh given to burdening its streets with statues, there was one other exception in addition to the matriarchal Queen - the poet Burns. Also in bronze and by the sculptor D.W. Stevenson, Scotland's national bard has stood at the east end of Bernard Street since 1898. Stevenson's name can be read on the panels (presented by William Tulloch and Robert Meikle) representing scenes from Burns's poems on the plinth.

The monument was commissioned by the Leith Burns Appreciation Society to commemorate his, admittedly rather tenuous, connections with the port where the locally brewed ale of Archibald Younger is said to have met with his unqualified approval. The annual celebration in Leith of Burns Night on 25th January, however, long ago became so well established as to justify in itself this well-placed and seemly representation of the poet which is without doubt an adornment to its surroundings.

A further statue had been proposed in 1850, the intention having been to erect 'a working men's memorial to Sir Robert Peel'. The Leith Town Council minutes record that the Provost 'had requested heads of the principal establishments employing workmen in the town to meet him'. But the scheme was quickly abandoned as, 'none of them having attended, he did not consider it advisable to call a public meeting.'

A small memorial to a building, easily missed by the passer-by, still survives on the wall of a modern house in the Kirkgate just before that truncated and redeveloped street, once the throbbing heart of old Leith, merges into Giles Street below Trinity House. Behind the front gardens can be seen a panel with a representation of the quaint and arcaded building called by John Russell in *The Story of Leith* 'the supposed Cant's Ordinary' and the inscription:

> On this site stood an ancient Tavern and
> Hostelry visited by Queen Mary, Oliver

Cromwell, Charles II and many notable French
Refugees. Much frequented by the elite
of the 16 & 17 centuries. Also a favourite
resort of Edinburghers and Leith cronies.

Demolished 1888

There are, however, reasons for believing that William
Cant's Hostelry, dating from the sixteenth century, was a
different building. An old account credits him with
presiding over one of the oldest houses in Leith and with
earning 'a certain recognition by the fact that when the
Earls of Argyle and Athole took the field against the Earl
of Morton for the possession of the person of James
VI in 1578, wiser counsels prevailed, and instead of
bloodshed a banquet took place in Cant's Hostelry, and
all went as merry as a marriage bell'. When Kinnaird's
Buildings, the substantial block which replaced the hostelry depicted, was pulled down, the panel was preserved
and incorporated in the row of 1960s housing which is a
far cry from the old thrang and closely built-up main-
street which was the Kirkgate that, with its shops and
houses and its narrow lanes and closes, thrust its way
down to Tolbooth Wynd (demolished at the same time as
the Kirkgate) in the not-so-distant past, the only original
buildings left on their foundations being Trinity House
and South Leith Parish Church.

The building in which Sir John Gladstone was born has
been lang syne swept away but a plaque at the corner of
King Street and Great Junction Street marks the

Site of birthplace of
Sir John Gladstone, Bart. 1764
Father of the
Rt. Hon. William Ewart Gladstone, M.P.
Born 1809
Four times Prime Minister

The fine Georgian merchant's house of Smith's Place which stands facing Leith Walk and which has been in commercial occupation for many years.

This tablet erected by
the Leith Liberal Club 1909

Fairly recently a familiar landmark has disappeared from the streets of Trinity, the Royal Forth Yacht Club having removed its large 'Siege of Leith' anchor from Boswall Road to its new location at Granton Harbour.

On a Saturday evening in February 1850 a spectacular fire occurred in the warehouses of the manufacturing chemists J. & R. Raimes, predecessors of Raimes Clark & Co Ltd, off Leith Walk, when the efforts of firemen to save Smith's Place, the still extant house (built by the merchant James Smith in 1812) in the short street of that

The rear view of Smith's Place showing the iron stair which led originally to the garden.

name which was then the home of Mr John Raimes, were, happily, successful. The fire engines of the Leith police had to be augmented by those of Leith Fort, which were operated by a company of Artillery, and of Edinburgh Castle, and the Queen's Bays stationed at Piershill Barracks sent the cavalry to their assistance. It took them five hours to get the outbreak under control, by which time the roof had fallen in and the contents of the warehouses had been totally destroyed. The back of the splendid Smith's Place villa, which was originally the garden front, has an attractive iron stair, parallel with the building, leading up to a door above the basement. The notable interior includes a geometric stair and the friezes are a feature of the groundfloor rooms.

Burning buildings were not a new phenomenon, but in 1901 the discovery of gold beneath the pavements of the port was unprecendented. When a new addition to Leith Hospital was being built in King Street the workmen engaged in excavating the ground for the foundations came across a small piece of quartz containing the unexpected substance. This was soon being exaggerated into 'gold fever in Leith', and the local newspaper cautioned its readers that 'a few ounces of gold-bearing quartz do not make a goldfield'. On being assayed in Edinburgh it was found to contain only a small quantity of the precious metal, and further digging produced nothing more newsworthy than the quartz itself, fragments of which were distributed as curios. The Crown authorities, however, made known to the Hospital Directors their intention of claiming all gold discovered in their ground in King Street which, as it happened, overlay beds of auriferous quartz. The Directors' reply brought the 'Klondike' excitement to an end as quickly as it had begun. They were not, they said, carrying on mining operations and, as the area would shortly be covered over with cement foundations, they 'would not take any further action in the matter'.

Trinity was exceptional in the large number of burglaries committed there in the years immediately preceding the First World War and one, in particular, may be worth recording. In 1912 thieves broke into a house in Primrose Bank Road, stealing a variety of valuables including some of the owner's wearing apparel. But they were soon discovered, and apprehended, lording it along the streets of Leith in ill-fitting morning coats and ostentatiously carrying silver-topped canes, like Daft Meg and her mother, in their borrowed finery, in John Galt's *Annals of the Parish!*

CHAPTER 8

Sea-Bathing and Swimming Baths

IN 1776 the dwellinghouse attached to a brickfield on the north side of the public way later to be known as Prospect Bank Road was advertised as being 'nigh the sea for bathing' notwithstanding that the sea was a full half-mile away. It represented, no doubt, the early burgeoning of a belief in the therapeutic value of sea air in general and sea water in particular and was to be followed by a multiplicity of similar recommendations and inducements in the succeeding century after the successful introduction of bathing machines which made their first appearance in Leith in 1761 and could be hired at the beach.

The Chain Pier in Trinity, latterly a popular resort of swimmers, had an existence of nearly eighty years before it was broken up, in October 1898, by a north-easterly gale which had raged unabated for three nights and days. Only a few splintered piles were left and they also were to vanish in the course of time. The water at Leith being too shallow for steam-driven packet boats, it was built after steam navigation was brought to the Firth of Forth. The small craft that had carried passengers out to the packets were often dangerously overcrowded and the pier provided greater safety as well as more convenience.

The structure, five hundred feet in length and with a breadth of just four feet, was opened on 14th August 1821, and for the occasion Trinity was *en fête*. A grand procession started from Trinity Hotel and proceeded to the end of the Pier where the whole party piled aboard two steamers, accompanied by 'a band of music', for an inaugural sail, and salutes were fired from another two vessels in the Firth. On disembarking, the boat party, consisting of three hundred gentlemen, sat down to a cold collation provided by Mr Maclaren of the Trinity Hotel in

103

The Old Chain Pier at Trinity as it was represented, until recently, above the door of the Chain Pier Inn.

a tent set up on a platform at the end of the Pier. The purpose for which it was built and so triumphantly 'launched', however, was to be short-lived, for in 1838 the steam packets abandoned Trinity for the new facilities at Granton.

The Pier was owned by the Alloa Steam Packet Company but now passed into the hands of John Greig, a man of great energy and enterprise, who fitted it up with 'dressing boxes' for sea-bathers. Women had apparently not yet taken up the sport of swimming as the bathers, who were charged one penny to use the Pier, were exclusively male. As a concession, trains ran every morning from Waverley, through the Scotland Street Tunnel, to Trinity Station just above the Pier for the benefit of early swim-

mers. A boat was always in attendance in case of accidents
and competitions and life-saving exhibitions attracted large
numbers of spectators.

After Greig's death it came into the possession of Mr
Eckford and subsequently of his son (who was probably
the Mr Walter Eckford who, with Mrs Eckford, was at
Beach House and Trinity Baths, which will be referred to
later, in 1875). The Pier then became the property of
the Colonial Life Assurance Company which later amalgamated with the Standard Life Office. They appointed a
caretaker who remained in charge until the storm of 1898,
an event the company may not altogether have regretted as
the Pier was in point of fact a rather insubstantial structure
in constant need of expensive maintenance and repair.
Consequently the spot soon began to lose its popularity
with bathers and swimmers, and a further disincentive was
the amount of sewage entering the water from both sides
of the Firth of Forth. There was no call, in these circumstances, for the Chain Pier to be rebuilt.

Many of the Pier's most regular swimmers were
employed in the shops and business premises of the city,
and the story of one of them has been preserved. He was
an Englishman called Mr Waterston who was an assistant
at Renton's, a drapery establishment in Princes Street. On
New Year's Night in 1857 he was returning, rather later
than usual, to his home on the South Side by way of the
Mound when, about midnight, he was attacked by a gang
of drunken hooligans. In his efforts to break free he drew
a knife from his pocket and had the misfortune to kill one
of his assailants. Going straight to the police station in the
High Street, he reported what had taken place, but the law
had to take its course and he was later tried for
manslaughter at the High Court. As he had an un-
blemished character and reputation he was honourably
acquitted, but left Edinburgh shortly after.

Indoor swimming baths reached the climax of their
popularity in the mid-nineteenth century and, like their

Georgian predecessors, the early Victorians patronised the baths at Seafield which had been built in 1813. In the 1850s the nearby Forthfield Baths were opened to meet clamant public demand and the present red sandstone Victoria Baths (later the Leith Corporation Baths where structural problems, raising doubts about their future, have recently been discovered) in Junction Place were built in 1899 by the architect George Simpson, son of the better-known James Simpson who a few years earlier had designed the old Council Chamber, entered from Queen Charlotte Street, in Leith Town Hall. And at No 30 Trinity Crescent (now flatted but still known as Bath House) opposite the Chain Pier site and close to the corner of York Road, Trinity Baths provided a further alternative to the open Firth. A singular feature here was the method of bringing in the sea water from the Forth by means of a pump beneath the pavement. No trace of these baths is visible today.

Adjoining Leith Fort on the north side of the Water of Leith was Bathfield House, a tenement with stables and gardens built in 1784, for the accommodation of families with a predilection for sea-bathing, by Thomas Bonnar & Son, the interior decorators.

As a favoured location for open-air swimming and for in-door swimming baths, the rise in popularity of Portobello brought about the abandonment of Trinity and Leith. It became a competitor almost overnight and, as a local newspaper afterwards expressed it, 'Leith had to choose between industry and pleasure, and chose the former'.

Bathing, however, could at times turn out to be a more hazardous occupation than had been bargained for. In August 1864 the *Leith Burghs Pilot* reported the strange case of Edinburgh resident James Hall who was charged with 'bathing on the 22nd inst near the foot of Tower Street without a bathing machine in defiance of the bye-laws for the regulation of the town' of Leith. In mitigation

Beach House on the corner of Trinity Crescent and York Road with, next door on the right, Bath House where sea water from the Firth of Forth was used in the Trinity Swimming Baths.

of his offence, the accused 'said he was on his way from Edinburgh to Haddington and, as the day was very hot, went into the water thinking it would refresh him', quite unaware that he was breaking any law. In view of the fact that the prisoner had been locked up all night, and probably also as he wisely decided to plead guilty, he was dismissed with no more than an admonition.

CHAPTER 9

The Provosts of Leith

AFTER Leith became a separate burgh in its own right in 1833 it was well served during the eighty-seven years of its independence by its civic heads, many of them self-made men of great ability, intelligence and resource. Such, indeed, was its first provost, Adam White. Born at Gifford about the year 1760, he commenced business in Edinburgh, with capital amounting to just £50, at the age of fifteen. To begin with his youth and his small stature gave his customers the impression that he must be a junior employee and he was frequently told that they would prefer to settle their accounts with his master! These drawbacks notwithstanding, he soon achieved considerable success in the import and export market, buying timber and other products from the Baltic and sending out principally cured herring from the Port. He was provost from 1833-39, displaying much tact and judgment in the administration of public affairs, and was also director of the old Leith Banking Company and of several shipping companies as well. On his retirement from office Adam White was presented with his portrait, but declined the proffered knighthood. He died on 31st December 1843.

James Reoch, the son of James Reoch of Banffshire, who was born in the Port on 6th November 1768, succeeded Adam White as the second provost of Leith (which included Trinity). In 1782 he was apprenticed to Charles Cowan, a local merchant whose family were to become famous as paper manufacturers in the following century, and entered his permanent employment five years later at an annual salary of £20 together with bed and board. On becoming a partner a few years later he took the time-honoured rags-to-riches route by marrying Isabella Cowan, the daughter of the senior partner, and

Top Left The first Provost of Leith, Adam White. He was elected in 1833 when Leith became a separate burgh. (Photograph by courtesy of Edinburgh City Libraries).

Top Right James Reoch, the second Provost of Leith. He had the unexpected honour of receiving the young Queen Victoria when she arrived at Granton on her first state visit to Scotland in 1842. (Photograph by courtesy of Edinburgh City Libraries).

The Leith wine merchant Thomas Hutchison, the third Provost of Leith, who acquired through his wife a link with the Emperor Nicholas of Russia. (Photograph by courtesy of Edinburgh City Libraries).

became a Burgher and Guild Brother of Leith in right of his wife in 1797. In 1803 he was admitted as a member of the Edinburgh Merchant Company and appointed Quarter-Master of the Royal Leith Volunteers by George III. When his successor, George IV, landed at the Shore in 1822 Reoch was among the first to greet the King, and later, having been elected provost in 1839, he received Queen Victoria and Prince Albert during their visit to Edinburgh in 1842. He died on 22nd November 1845, two weeks after demitting office as provost and retiring from public life, and was buried in South Leith Churchyard where a handsome monument was erected to his memory.

The third provost of the burgh was Thomas Hutchison who was born in Kinghorn in 1796 and attended Burntisland Grammar School where he met Thomas Carlyle, the future 'sage of Chelsea'. He started his business career in the employment of George Young & Co, wine merchants in Leith, where he became a partner. Leaving in 1825 to found his own business, he set up the firm of Hutchison & Co which became one of the oldest wholesale wine merchants' establishments in Leith. He was provost from 1845 to 1848, and it was at his instigation that the 'pestilential open ditches' then running through the Links were filled in and the common good greatly improved. In 1842 when Queen Victoria and Prince Albert arrived at Granton, at six in the morning, for their first official visit to Scotland after her coronation, it was by the Lord Provost of Edinburgh, Sir James Forrest, that she had expected to be received. In the event, however, this honour devolved upon Provost Reoch and the magistrates of the port of Leith. At 2 am a messenger was directed to the house in Bernard Street of the then Bailie Hutchison to announce the time when the Queen's visit was to commence. He at once sent him on to rouse the provost, dispatched his own servant to his fellow bailies and ordered his carriage to be made ready without delay. And so, when the Royal party stepped ashore, instead of the civic dignitaries of Edinburgh and the Royal Company of Archers (who were shortly afterwards, being then on a collision course with the Queen's own escort coming in the opposite direction, to be in total disarray), the provost and magistrates of Leith, all in good order and their robes of office, had pride of place in greeting the young monarch in her northern kingdom.

At the conclusion of his provostship Thomas Hutchison became the Town Council's representative on the Dock Commission. In 1852, at Hermitage House, he suffered an acute attack of peritonitis and died a few hours later. A stained glass window was subsequently installed in his memory in South Leith Parish Church. His wife was Jane Wylie, whose uncle, Sir James Wylie, Bart, was physician to the Emperor Nicholas of Russia, and his daughter, Isobel Wylie Hutchison, was well known as a writer on overseas travel with a special interest in the Arctic, its people and its plants.

Elected in his place was another Leith wine merchant, George Adinston M'Laren, who was provost from 1848 to 1851. A Liberal of the old Whig type, he became chairman of the Leith Liberal Committee and was a friend of Lords Murray (John A. Murray, the Lord Advocate), Rutherfurd, (Andrew Rutherfurd, advocate and Lord of Session, who owned and lived in Lauriston Castle from 1844 to 1854) and Moncrieff, the first three Members of Parliament for Leith Burghs. George M'Laren married Helen Borthwick, the daughter of John Borthwick of Crookston. The Edinburgh house of the Borthwicks of Crookston, built in 1770, is the only survivor of the eighteenth century villas of Lauriston and stands, with its back to the street, beside Chalmers Hospital. It was known as Lauriston Lodge and St. Catherine's Convent of Mercy was built in its grounds in 1860.

From 1851 to 1855 the provost of the Port was Robert Philip. Born in Fife, he had come to Leith about 1825. During his term of office the erection of 'drying poles' on the Links was the cause of considerable agitation in the community and eventually became the subject of litigation between the Council and the golfers. The latter being successful, the poles were removed from the ground. Philip's public life was unfortunately brought to an ignominious end in 1855 when he was sentenced to fifteen years transportation for indecent behaviour, although he was only required to serve a much shorter term. He died in Corstorphine in 1887.

Born (c 1800) and educated in Leith, James Taylor held the 'honourable office' of provost from 1855 to 1860. He had established an extensive corn merchants' business as the active partner in the firm of Taylor, Bruce & Co. and carried his strict, mercantile abhorrence of wasting time into the Council Chamber. Here he sat, pocket-watch in hand, suppressing all irrelevant discussion, with the result that meetings lasted, as a rule, not more than fifteen minutes! James Taylor, perhaps not surprisingly, was unmarried and died on 18th February 1890 aged eighty-nine.

William Lindsay, born in Coburg Street in 1819 and the son of a Leith shipmaster, was cast in a very different mould from that of his predecessors. He was articled to Alex. Simpson, SSC in Bernard Street, at an early age and practised as a solicitor in Leith for many years. An interest, possibly inherited from his father, in the sea, however, led him away from law and at the outbreak of the Crimean War he undertook the provision of steam transports for the use of the French and, in 1864, he withdrew entirely from the legal profession and devoted his energies to the business of shipping. He was elected provost in 1860 and remained in that position for the next six years.

His knowledge of law enabled him very expertly to frame the General Police and Improvement (Scotland) Act which was placed on the Statute Book in 1862 and was usually referred to as the 'Lindsay Act' in recognition of his work which was held in very high regard throughout the country. William Lindsay died on 20th February 1884, when a marble bust by Brodie was placed in his memory in Leith Town Hall.

From 1866 to 1875 the provostship was held by James Watt who had been born in Brechin in 1806 and who had entered the wine trade in the Port, eventually acquiring the business of J.A. Bertram in Quality Street (now Maritime Street). In 1869 he opened the new Albert Dock and was presented to Queen Victoria when she visited the Dock in 1872. He was elected three times as provost and died on 22nd December 1881.

John Henderson, MD, FRCSE, born near Jedburgh in 1818, was provost from 1875 to 1881. After spending some time in France, where he was engaged in literary work, he qualified in 1845 and, after assisting Dr Coldstream of Leith, built up a large medical practice of his own. It was only with considerable reluctance that he agreed to enter the Town Council in an attempt to remedy the squalid, miserable and insanitary conditions in the poorer part of the burgh, but his efforts bore fruit in the Leith Improvement Scheme which was implemented in 1878. His date of death does not appear to be known.

A junior clerk in the service of the Edinburgh Roperie Company in Leith, who later became manager of the business on the death of the proprietor, James Hay, was elected provost of the burgh in 1881 and remained in office until 1886. He was James Pringle, born in Edinburgh in 1822 and educated at the Royal High School. He died in December 1886 at his residence in Claremont Park beside the Links.

Provost Thomas Aitken, born at Dalmeny on 21st September 1832, held office from 1887 to 1893. After an apprenticeship with William Wilson of Swanfield Mills in Leith he entered into partnership with his brother-in-law as a wholesale provision and flour merchant under the firm name of Aitken & Wright in Charlotte Lane. During his period as provost Edinburgh made the first of its three

The penultimate Provost of Leith was Sir Malcolm Smith. He is seen here with George V during a visit by the King and Queen Mary to the Ex-Servicemen's Settlement at Earl Haig Gardens in 1923.

overtures to Leith to unite, along with Portobello, with the city. To this proposal Provost Aitken offered 'his most determined opposition' and the matter was dropped, at any rate for the time being. His date of death does not seem to have been recorded.

He was succeeded by John Bennet, born at Leith on 29th April 1820 and educated at Leith Fort School. He was apprenticed to a shipping company but 'ran away to

sea', although fifteen months later he decided to return. He
was the second provost to fight off Edinburgh's amalgamation blandishments when he took a deputation to London
to oppose the Bill, and during his provostship (1893-99)
North and South Leith were united for parochial purposes.
Sir Richard Mackie, whose life is outlined in *Traditions
of Trinity and Leith*, was provost from 1899 to 1908.
The penultimate provost of the Port was Sir Malcolm
Smith, KBE, who was a native of Shetland and subsequently represented Orkney and Shetland as a Member
of Parliament. He became managing director of a fish
curing and preserving business and, in 1898, created the
North British Cold Storage & Ice Company. He died at
his home, Clifton Lodge, No 3 Boswall Road in Trinity,
on 12th March 1935, having been provost from 1908 to
1917. Clifton Lodge, now in the ownership of the Church
of Scotland, was renamed Wallace House in 1977 after an
American, Dr George C. Wallace, whose generous be-
quest enabled the building to be purchased for use as
a children's home on their removal from Malta House
in Stockbridge which then became a Community Care
Rehabilitation Centre.

It fell to a native of the Port, John A. Lindsay, DL, JP,
a founder member of the firm of John & Charles Lindsay,
flour importers in Leith, to take office, in 1917, as the
fifteenth and last provost of the burgh. He too tried to
preserve the independence of the old seaport but the net
had been steadily closing, and, in 1920, after laying aside
the robes and insignia of the 'honourable office' in which
he was to have no successor, he was appointed Chairman
of the Leith Dock Commission and died on 21st April
1942.

E

CHAPTER 10

Prominent People and Local Characters

IT was the opinion of Sir Walter Scott that, next to the High Street and the Canongate of Edinburgh, the most interesting thoroughfare in Scotland was the Kirkgate. Along with the Shore and Tolbooth Wynd, it was certainly the most ancient in the port of Leith and also the street in which the more affluent of its citizens chose to live, the other two being largely given over to taverns, warehouses and stores. Here in the Kirkgate, between the mansions of those famous old Leith sea-dogs Sir Andrew Wood and Sir Andrew Barton in the reign of James III, was the house of Andrew Haliburton in the late sixteenth and early seventeenth centuries. Haliburton was a celebrated Scoto-Flemish merchant who lived principally at Middleburg where he was Conservator of Scots Privileges and a man of considerable influence and standing. Leith in his time (when the Scots were said to drink more claret than the English) was in constant trading communication with Bordeaux and the Garonne, but, besides wine, Haliburton dealt in a wide range of merchandise. He acted as agent for churchmen as well as laymen and with the piety that was then so integral a part of the Scottish character, the word 'Jhesus' was inscribed at the foot of all his accounts.

He maintained his family home in the Kirkgate till 1603, the date of the Union of the Crowns, when, following King James VI to London, such success attended his trading activities there that he was able to bequeath a profitable legacy to the present day and, indeed, the foreseeable future. The great modern banking house, known in the nineteenth century as Barclay & Co, was built on the sound financial foundations which were laid, three hundred and fifty years ago, by the grand old Kirkgate merchant, Andrew Haliburton.

John Taylor (1580 - 1653) was an English contemporary of Haliburton but one whose life and accomplishments were of a very different order. In addition to keeping a tavern in London Taylor was employed there as a Thames waterman as well and, as he also wrote pamphlets and doggerel verse, was known from his connection with the river as 'the Water-poet'. Walking from London to the Scottish capital in 1618 without a coin in his pockets, he described his experiences in *The Pennyles Pilgrimage* in which publication he also praised the beauty of the old town of Edinburgh. He mentions the warm welcome he received to Leith from Bernard Lindsay, a Groom of the Bedchamber to King James, and while there he met his fellow-countryman Ben Johnson, who was in the company of the Scottish poet Drummond of Hawthornden, in the Old Ship Tavern at the Shore. 'Honest Ben' gave Taylor 'a piece of gold of two and twenty shillings to drink the health of England' and the Water-poet later recalled the inn in one of his 'voluminous rhymes'.

Although local only in his early years, poor Andrew Macdonald should not be denied a place among the noteworthy characters of Leith in the eighteenth century. He was born at the 'foot of the Walk' in 1755, probably where the Star Music Hall, which later became a grain store, was subsequently built. The site and the area around it is better known today as the former Leith Central Station. His father was George Donald, a gardener. As a child, Andrew was seen as something of a prodigy, as 'one who was likely to shine in after life, particularly in the literary world'.

His parents encouraged him to seek ordination in the Scottish Episcopal Church in which he had been brought up, and he matriculated at Edinburgh University at a fairly early age. Taking deacon's orders about 1775, he was advised by the bishop, for reasons which have remained obscure, 'to prefix "Mac" to his name'. This he did and, as no vacant living was immediately available, he obtained a temporary 'preceptorship' in the family of the Oliphants of Gask. Two years later, however, for which purpose he now took priest's orders, he became pastor of the Episcopal community in Glasgow.

Five years afterwards, deciding at last to pursue the possibilities of authorship, he published *Velina—a Poetical Fragment* which was soon followed by a novel called *The Independent*. Undaunted by their failure, and having 'the spirit of "Persevere" in his veins', he went on to write *Vimonda*, a tragedy which, with a prologue by Henry Mackenzie, the author of *The Man of Feeling*, was produced at the Theatre Royal in Edinburgh and proved a considerable success. At that time, following the collapse of the Jacobite rebellions, the Episcopal Church in Scotland was in a depressed condition as the old members of that community were dying out and were not being replaced by their descendants. As a consequence Andrew Macdonald's congregation had become so small that there was no longer 'a living in the charge'. So he left the clerical profession and returned to Edinburgh where he embarked, with sanguine expectations, on a career in literature.

Before leaving Glasgow he took unto him a wife—'a chaste, homely maid-servant from the house where he had lodged'. To his sorrow this was seen as a degrading marriage for a clergyman and he 'was assailed on every hand by those whom he imagined would have befriended him'. Perhaps in a gesture of self-defence, he rented a large house and proceeded to furnish it. But this was well beyond his means and, to escape the demands of his creditors as well as the taunts of his former friends, he resolved to seek literary work in London, leaving his mother, whom he revered, in charge of his affairs in Edinburgh.

To begin with all went well. The fame of *Vimonda* had gone before him and in the summer of 1787, soon after his arrival, it was produced 'with much splendour' and was an immediate success which was repeated the following year. He now became over-optimistic and, elated with hopes of fame and independence, wrote to Mr Stewart, a musicseller (and his only sincere and trustworthy friend and mentor) in Edinburgh who had 'advanced him money', in high hopes of being able to pay off all his debts. In three weeks, he said, he expected to be 'flourishing at the Haymarket Theatre'.

Andrew Macdonald's health, however, had suffered from his many problems and financial difficulties, and a few months after writing the letter he died—a victim of misfortune and a weak constitution—at the age of thirty-three, in 1788, leaving a widow and one child.

For a short time before his death he 'had amused London', under the name of Matthew Bramble, with a number of burlesque and humorous poems which attracted the notice of Isaac Disraeli, the author and father of Lord Beaconsfield, the Victorian Statesman and Prime Minister, who wrote of him:

> One evening I saw a tall, famished, melanchony man enter a bookseller's shop, his hat flopped over his eyes and his whole frame evidently feeble from exhaustion and utter misery. The bookseller enquired how he proceeded with the tragedy. 'Do not talk to me about tragedy', he replied, 'I have indeed more tragedy than I can bear at home!' This man was Matthew Bramble, the writer of comic poetry. He died, in extreme poverty, in Kentish Town in London.

In the *Leith Observer* 'Restalrig' recalled the circumstances of Macdonald's life as having some similarities to his own. He too had been born in Leith and had tried to live in London by the aid of his pen and, 'when things looked their blackest, Dame Fortune came to his aid and thrust in his way an actress' who, anxious to 'get off the ligitimate stage and on to the music halls', asked him to write for her 'a burlesque sketch'. He did so. It was

F

produced at the Marylebone Music Hall on August Bank Holiday 1896. And he was glad to say it was successful. He felt affinity with the Leith preacher, poet and dramatist of the previous century, a copy of whose works, he said, had been placed in the Advocates' Library in Edinburgh. In 1790 a volume of his sermons had been published posthumously and had been 'an enormous success'. It may be hoped that his family benefited, as no doubt they did, but it had come too late to revive the fortunes or prolong the life of Andrew Macdonald. Had it done so, Leith might have remembered him as it remembered The Rev John Home, the author of *Douglas*, with whom he had at one time been not unfavourably compared. *Douglas* has been revived in recent years. Could the same thing happen to *Vimonda*?

In March 1910 the death was announced in the *Leith Observer* of Mr Thomas Armit of the East Coast Salvage Co Limited, who had died at his home, Belrorie Lodge, No 11 Zetland Place in Trinity. He had 'made a new era in the work of refloating stranded ships' and, as he was 'called whenever a difficult bit of salvage work was required... his name was known throughout the maritime world.'

Thomas Napier Armit, the son of a shipbuilder and contractor, was born in Montrose in 1846 and entered the salvage business at the beginning of his career, first in Dundee and then in Leith. He refloated vessels in every estuary and channel of the British coasts, saving cargoes which would otherwise have been lost, and carried out salvage work around the world. After the Tay Bridge disaster, when the central spans collapsed in a gale while a train was crossing on 28th December 1879, Thomas Armit was brought in to work on the wreckage. Although still young and comparatively inexperienced, he was able to raise the engine, which was still in running order, the carriages and as much of the structure of the bridge as could be brought to the surface.

In addition to his very specialised sphere of work, he had many literary interests and was known to many as, in particular, a 'Shakespearean scholar'.

Trinity can lay claim to another member of the acting profession. On 9th February 1924 a columnist in the same newspaper wrote that 'Mr Lamont Dickson, who comes to Edinburgh next week to play at the King's Theatre in *The Outsider*, has a Leith connection inasmuch as his father, Mr Lamont Dickson, Civil Engineer, resides at "Fernlea" in Zetland Place, in Trinity. Mr Dickson, jnr, was educated at George Watson's College and some years before the war went to London to enter upon a stage career. He soon impressed Mr Robert Courtneidge, for after three weeks in the chorus [of a musical comedy] Mr Dickson had a chance to play the leading part.' Later, after other similar engagements, 'on the sudden illness of the late Louis Bradfield, who was playing a leading role, Mr Dickson undertook the part', and shortly afterwards 'resolved to leave musical comedy and devote himself to the legitimage drama in which he quickly established himself as a character actor.' He 'joined the London Scottish on the outbreak of the late war and subsequently obtained a commission in the RAF.'

With his brother John, he grew up in Trinity and the latter part of his life was spent in South Africa.

'Weel kent' in Leith in his day and generation (which coincided with the rise in national significance of the Faculty of Medicine at Edinburgh University and its concomitant sins of omission that led to the unbridled activities of the 'body snatchers') was the local character called Peter Brand who was always known as Patie. As many farm animals were kept on their premises by the indwellers of Edinburgh and Leith, Patie was by no means alone in being the possessor of a sow; what was unusual was his method of disposing of it, and turning it to his own financial advantage, when the creature died. Its demise took place, apparently, on a dark and wintry afternoon, when it was promptly packed and parcelled in a tea chest and conveyed by its optimistic owner to Surgeon Square for Dr Knox, the anatomist, who was soon to fall from grace when he failed to enquire regarding the source of Burke and Hare's too-frequent deliveries to the same address. Ringing the bell without a qualm, he asked £10 for what he called 'a good corp'. It being late in the day, no questions were asked and Patie was given 'a line' to Dr Knox at Newington, acknowledging receipt of the box. So Patie proceeded to the doctor's house. The 'corp' had died the previous night, he said, and was 'in good condition'. Five pounds were handed over at the door and he was told to call at Surgeon Square for the balance in the morning. Delighted at this satisfactory oucome of his 'practical joke', Patie went home in the highest of spirits, only stopping in Leith Walk for a celebratory gill at the Half Way House.

In the meantime the box had been opened and the hoax discovered, and the culprit was confronted by the police before he had time to order a second gill. But he had his answer ready, as usual. 'I never told you it was a human corp', he said. 'The next time you take in an "object", it might be worth your while to speer if it be sow or man!'.

Peter Brand was a carter and casual labourer by trade, and on loading a Leith sloop with soot on one occasion was hailed by a passing Irishman looking for work. 'Can you tramp soot?', cried Patie ashore. The reply was a flying leap from the quayside into the 'yielding cargo' beneath which the over-zealous Pat at once disappeared from sight. It so happened that a chimney sweep was still on board and he obligingly, though also at some risk, plunged his ladder down the hatchway and brought the blackened Irishman up to the daylight and the astonished bystanders' gaze. Whether he 'tramped soot' after such an experience is not related!

The escapades of Peter Brand were recorded by 'the illustrious poet and song writer', Robert Gilfillan, otherwise known as 'the Poet of Leith', who called him 'a Coalhill Dandie Dinmont' who, though frequently in court for petty offences, appears to have been held in some affection by the Leith authorities. Not wishing to send him to prison, the Magistrate once asked him to look around to see if there was not a friend who would advance him half-a-crown to pay his fine. 'There's jist yin, yer honour', Patie said, 'with the means an' hert to help me, but I jist canna muster courage to ask him.' 'Point him out to me', replied Bailie Young, 'and I'll ask him for you.' 'Then ye must jist ask yoursel', my lord', came the answer, 'for there's no ither in the hale court as wad gie me a groat to save me from the gallows.' The compliment had the desired effect, but he was told he must pay it back. 'I hope I'll be a long while yer honour's debtor', said the grateful Patie, but soon after he was back at the bar again.

The last appearance in court of Peter Brand was on 19th September 1832 when he was charged with assault. But he died in hospital shortly afterwards, having fallen victim to an outbreak of cholera in the Port.

CHAPTER 11

Streams and Drainage

IN the early years of the history of Leith the water supply was obtained from the streams and burns that once crossed the open countryside, the Water of Leith being the principal source with the Greenside and Broughton Burns contributing as well. The Water of Leith, rising in the Pentland Hills and approximately twenty miles in length, flowed, as most of the Edinburgh watercourses do, in a south-westerly to a north-easterly direction and reached Leith, by way of what later became Stockbridge, Canonmills and Warriston, beneath the present Newhaven Road and Great Junction Street. From here it ran by Coalhill and the Shore to its estuary on the Firth of Forth. This formed the natural harbour around which developed the original Leith (or, as it was then called, Inverleith) village.

The Greenside Burn, rising on Calton Hill, ran, eastwards of Leith Walk, towards the sea, then altered course in a westerly direction and joined the Broughton Burn (which rose at Beaverhall), the combined waters of these two streams then flowing into the Water of Leith itself. The course of the Broughton Burn carried it through the grounds of Pilrig House and, as it had become seriously polluted, it was led into a culvert during the laying out as a cemetery of the grounds of the demolished Rosebank House in the 1840s.

Across the Wardie Muir, on which Trinity was later to be built around Trinity Mains, the farm of the Masters and Mariners of Trinity House of Leith, flowed the Anchorfield Burn. Emerging to the north of Bangholm Bower, it ran to the south of East Trinity Road, took a southerly loop in the area of Newhaven Road and then, turning in a north-easterly direction, entered the sea at the eastern end of Hawthornvale where land reclamation has subsequently

Sir Alexander Morison, MD (1779-1866) by Richard Dadd. Sir Alexander Morison specialised in mental disorders and was a Fellow of the Royal Colleges of Physicians of Edinburgh and London. Painted by the Victorian 'faery' painter Richard Dadd who was one of his patients, this view also shows Anchorfield House, in which Alexander Morison, who was knighted in 1838, was born. The house stands behind the two Newhaven fishwives. Sir Alexander died in Scotland and was buried at Currie. (Photograph by courtesy of The Scottish National Portrait Gallery).

created the western end of the Dock area at the junction of Newhaven Place and Lindsay Road. The long-demolished Anchorfield House once stood at the point of outfall of the Burn. In the Leith Town Council minutes of February 1851 it is recorded that the Council agreed to memorialise the Trustees of roads for the County of Edinburgh to take steps for repairing the road along the beach between Leith Fort and Anchorfield without delay. The sea was a frequent creator of hazards on coastal roads and probably necessitated this (by no means the only)

One of the two remaining guardhouses inside the old walls of Leith Fort. The walls still retain the original entrance flanked by two narrower arched entrances for foot soldiers, but the large housing complex of Fort House, behind, has replaced the other buildings.

request for urgent maintenance measures to be undertaken.

In old Leith the water was once more close at hand than it has since become. The original Signal Tower (which has been described as being 'like a Border peel tower with little port-holes at the top') stood near the junction of the Kirkgate and the Tolbooth Wynd, but as the sea receded it was left too far from the Firth to be of any use. So the former windmill, used in the production of rape-seed oil, at the Shore was adapted for the purpose. (It has been adapted again, as flats, in recent years.) The upper story dates from the late nineteenth century.

Leith Fort was built in 1780 (by James Craig

The Granton-Leith intercepting sewer under construction.

(1744-95), the architect of the New Town of Edinburgh) a year after the John Paul Jones scare when that adventurous Scot who earned for himself the title of Father of the US Navy appeared with several ships and aggressive intentions in the roads of Leith but was blown out of the Firth by a severe gale. Built in haste to counter any possible repetition, its guns were in action on the fourth of June in 1781 – but only to mark the birthday of King George III! The entrance to the Fort (the remains of which are still in existence in North Fort Street) was on the sea road which was subject to frequent erosion by the tide. Originally, the lands of Bonnington stretched from the Water of Leith to the Anchorfield Burn.

Further to the west the Wardie Burn flowed through West and East Pilton and then turned north-east to enter the Forth eastwards of the Eastern Breakwater of Granton Harbour.

These streams, like many others throughout the city, are still there but, having been culverted in the nineteenth century and become, in some cases, part of Edinburgh's sewerage system, are now running underground. In order to use the natural drainage of the area the pipes were laid, as far as possible, on the line of the existing watercourses, and throughout much of the Edinburgh system rain water, as a diluting agent, is directed into the sewers. Under normal weather conditions the conduits have sufficient capacity for both, but during a storm the diluted effluent may be passed, by overflow outlets constructed for the purpose, into the Water of Leith where the swollen stream provides additional dilution. Although the river is now considered to be clean, and anglers can frequently be seen along its banks, the river water itself should not be drunk.

In medieval times the Old Town shared the fate of all such gathered communities in its intermittent outbreaks of epidemic disease, particularly cholera, due mainly to the lack of proper drainage. (The last cholera epidemic in Edinburgh and Leith was in 1866 and there was a cholera alert as late as 1893, the year in which an old wooden building on the west pier of Leith, which had been used for over twenty years as a cholera isolation hospital, was closed down.) It was not until the middle of the eighteenth century that the Nor' Loch, a repository for generations of all detritus, dead cats and general garbage, was drained, and much later, and with difficulty, that the South, or Burgh, Loch was freed from mud and water.

To deal with pollution in the Water of Leith legislation was introduced in 1854 and again a decade later. As a consequence a new sewer, which intercepted existing drains, was laid as far up as Roseburn, the Forth estuary being its point of discharge to the sea. Intercepting sewers were laid from time to time thereafter in order to collect the discharges from small drains which had led separately to outlets on the foreshore. Commissioners were appointed

Seafield screening plant.

to administer the Water of Leith under the terms of the
Water of Leith Purification and Sewerage Act of 1889 and
a trunk sewer from Leith to Balerno was constructed soon
afterwards to collect all waste pollutants then going directly into the river. Its line is straighter than the line of
the river up to Stockbridge but from Stockbridge to
Balerno it follows the watercourse. At the point of outfall
its diameter is five feet but this reduces to ten inches at the
summit of the gradient. (The angle of the gradient varied
throughout Edinburgh, as did the depth at which the pipes
were laid, some being well below the level of the watercourse.)

At the beginning of the nineteenth century the Foul
Burn, an open sewer, was formed to carry effluent from
the existing Old Town drains to the Firth of Forth, and
Craigentinny sewage farm was laid out, in the form of
irrigation channels branching off from the Foul Burn,
across the marshland of Craigentinny Meadows. Part of
this site is now covered by Craigentinny Golf Course and

The weir on the Water of Leith which once powered the millwheel at the now demolished Bonnington Mill.

the rest, to the south of Restalrig, has been built up. The Foul Burn was a disease-carrying and insanitary waterway and the local children were warned, although not always with much success, to keep well away from it. This unsatisfactory state of affairs was remedied, somewhat late in the day, in 1922 by the construction of the Craigentinny Sewer from Seafield up to Clockmill Lane.

Also in the nineteenth century a covered channel known as the Greenside Burn Sewer was run from the north-west end of Great Junction Street south-west to Duke Street and then south to serve the area between Leith Walk and Easter Road. It finally ascended the short valley of the Greenside Burn at Calton Hill. The Wardie Burn Sewer was constructed in 1925 and a sewer also follows the line of the Anchorfield Burn.

During 1934 and 1935 the policy of constructing intercepting sewers 'was applied on a much bigger scale by grouping together some of the main sewers and bring-

The former railway viaduct over the Water of Leith at Bonnington in 1974. The house of Bonnyhaugh is in the background and part of the viaduct had already been demolished.

ing their points of discharge to new outfalls. Sewers serving Granton, Wardie, Trinity and Newhaven were thus brought together to a point of discharge out from McKelvie Parade' at the junction of Trinity and Granton. 'Before entering the new outfall, all the effluents pass through a vertical screening plant where solids are intercepted, then disintegrated and passed to the sea. The outfall itself extends some three hundred yards below low water mark and thus clear of Newhaven and Granton Harbours.' (Main Drainage of the City of Edinburgh, Edinburgh Corporation, 1955.)

In 1936 the Trinity Screening Plant was built at the outfall of the Wardie Burn Sewer, the Granton Screening Plant was constructed at Caroline Park in 1930 and the

Seafield Screening Plant dates from 1945. Four years later a further sewer was connected to the screening plant at Seafield and the outfall here consists of a steel pipe seven feet in diameter which is encased in concrete and extends into the estuary four hundred and fifty-five yards below low water mark. An important addition to the system is the Seafield Sewage Treatment Works opened in 1978 at Seafield Road.

At Redbraes, near the broad weir, or dam, on the Water of Leith which once served the Bonnington Mill lade, is a tall, brick sewer vent which rises up unexpectedly from the ground like a strayed and forgotten factory chimney. The lade ran eastwards towards the mill where it turned the wheel, then under Newhaven Road and back to the river.

The Water of Leith, Edinburgh's river, has been called a 'willing drudge'. It has provided the power for driving grain mills, paper mills and snuff mills as well as water for tanneries and other light industries along its banks; it has played a major role in drainage and sewerage for the city's population; and it was transformed in recent years from a contaminated watercourse into a clear-flowing stream in which fish (the Water of Leith is stocked annually with trout) could be found as far down as Leith itself. But this state of affairs is now undergoing a change for the worse and the Leith stretches of the river are polluted once again. This is due, in part, to the closure of the lock gates, installed as long ago as 1969, to maintain a high and constant water level in the Western Harbour, which prevents the regular cleansing of the lower reaches by the tide. Renewed efforts are consequently being made to have the Water of Leith repurified as a safe and usable natural recreational resource.

Fresh water, prior to the establishment in Edinburgh of a Water Company in 1819, was obtained from public wells and also from wells sunk on private property (as at St. Marie's in East Trinity Road) as well as from the Water of Leith and other smaller streams. The supply from public

The columnar supports of the old railway viaduct which still stand in the Water of Leith to the west of Bonnington.

wells was augmented from time to time by water brought in in pipes from Comiston, Swanston and Crawley and conveyed to the still extant (but rebuilt) reservoir at the top of Castle Hill. From there it was led to the wells in the Royal Mile a few of which, although they no longer function as wells, can still be seen. The water caddies who climbed the long stairs of the many-storeyed Old Town 'lands', each one 'dripping all the way', according to an old description, 'like a thawing icicle', obtained their water from these public wells and sold it for a penny a barrel to those who were too incapacitated or too old to bring it up themselves. In the outlying areas beyond the city boundaries the Water of Leith, the streams and the private wells appear to have sufficed.

In the middle of the eighteenth century, however, the rather low quality water from Lochend Loch was utilised as a (somewhat inadequate) supply of fresh water for the town of Leith when the growing population was giving rise to an increased demand.

CHAPTER 12

Trade and Industry

FOR the ancient craft of tanning the banks of the Water of Leith provided an ideal situation and many tanneries were to be found along its length, that belonging to Messrs White, Burns & Co, skinners, tanners and wool merchants, being a prominent landmark until the recent past at the Bonnington end of Newhaven Road.

The skin works and warehouses occupied the long, three-storeyed building, much of it once ivy-covered, and made copious industrial use of the river until their closure in 1972. Opposite, on the west side of Newhaven Road, the row of tenements called, after the founder of the company, Burns Place, has outlived its original purpose of housing the skin workers and a small, square panel carved with the tools of the tanning trade can still be seen on the wall between the first and second floors.

Behind Burns Place, Bonnington Mills and the early seventeenth century house of Bonnyhaugh were the property of White, Burns & Co at least until the 1930s as it was here that the bleachfields of the Bonnyhaugh linen manufactory had been purchased for the establishment of his business, exactly a hundred years previously, by Robert Burns.

White, Burns & Co amalgamated with the Edinburgh tanners Robert Legget & Sons and the business was transferred to Fife. The splendid old Bonnington building was vacated in 1972 and, although it is now in the possession of J.H. Sankey & Son Ltd, Builders' Merchants, only the facade has been retained.

Since Walter Chepman set up his press, the first in Scotland, in the Old Town of Edinburgh in the reign of James IV, the city has been justly famed for the number, and the high quality, of its printers. No exception was the

The vacated Bonnington Tannery in Newhaven Road as it appeared in 1975.

well-known Leith firm of Printers and Lithographers, W. & A.K. Johnston Ltd, whose Edina Works were for many years to be found in Easter Road and who, after small and unpretentious beginnings, had an interesting and illustrious history.

In 1825 William Johnston (1802-88), the founder of the enterprise, set up a hand-press at No 6 Hill Square in Edinburgh and began in a modest way as a steel-plate and copper-plate printer, moving in the following year, when he was joined by his younger brother Alexander Keith, to 160 High Street in the Old Town.

The venture soon became a prosperous undertaking, so successful in fact that the brothers were appointed engravers to 'His Reigning Majesty King William IV' in 1834, and three years later, on the death of the 'Sailor King', to Queen Victoria. They removed the same year to No 4 St. Andrew Square. By then they had added map making to their activities and it was this departure that led not only to the greater advancement of their business but to international recognition as well, Keith Johnston becoming one of the leading men of science of his day. Honours were showered upon him by geographical societies around the world, the degree of LLD was conferred on him by the University of Edinburgh and he was given the additional appointment of Geographer to Her Majesty the Queen.

William Johnston, having become Lord Provost of Edinburgh in 1848, was later knighted by Queen Victoria at Holyrood Palace. He retired in 1867 after forty-two years' service in the flourishing business he himself had founded and his name is commemorated in Johnston Terrace behind the Castle rock.

A third brother, Thomas Johnston, had been taken into the firm in 1852 and in 1879, the St. Andrew Square premises being by then too small, the Edina Works were built in Edina Place off Easter Road. It was here that the maps which were so widely used in schools were prepared and printed.

Keith Johnston had died in 1871, and on the death of Thomas in 1901 the firm became a limited company. The Edina Works were closed in 1970.

The house called Ashbrook, at the western end of Ferry Road, was the home of Sir Robert Maule, the proprietor, well known in his day, of Messrs Robert Maule & Son in the premises later occupied by Binns and now by Fraser's Department Store at the west end of Princes Street. In 1872 Robert Maule and his son moved to Leith from his native Kincardine-on-Forth where he had been in business for some years as a draper and general furnisher. His Leith premises, known as The Popular House, were at Nos 74,

75 and 76 Tolbooth Wynd and his advertisements appeared regularly in the *Leith Burghs Pilot*. In 1881, in addition to fur-lined cloaks and 'a great Lot of Ulsters', he proffered his potential customers such bargains as 'a lot of pure coloured silks at 1/6 per yard', 'a Bale of heavy Stockinette tweed at 8½ d a yard, being very near half price', and 'Real Brussel carpets 2/8 per yard'. Goods were delivered by their own vans throughout Edinburgh twice a day and, in Leith and district, every hour! The business remained here until 1893 when it was transferred to Princes Street.

His prestigious residence of Ashbrook is an ornate Victorian pile, with statutory tower, in sombre-coloured stone and with a hint of Italian edifices of similar design, and has for many years been a Salvation Army Eventide Home. Its western neighbour is the Scots Baronial Wardieburn, of corresponding vintage, which is the property of D.S. Crawford, the biscuit manufacturers.

Sir Robert Maule retired to a house in Corstorphine called The Lea where he died, aged 69, in 1926. In the report of his death in the *Edinburgh and Leith Observer* he is described as a generous benefactor and a respected citizen.

The Norwegian name of Salvesen has been well known in Leith and Trinity since the middle of the nineteenth century when Salve Christian Fredrik Salvesen (1827-1911) made the sea-crossing to Leith at the beginning of his career in maritime commerce. The firm of Salvesen & Turnbull had been established there in 1846 by his brother Theodore after his tentative initial entrance into shipbuilding, at Grangemouth, in the early 1840s had proved successful. Scope for new industrial development in Norway was, until later in the century, severely restricted by the state of the economy and the only possibilities of advancement for the country's enterprising youth lay beyond its shores. So Theodore Salvesen took Christian, his younger brother, who already had had some experience, into the new Leith company, first as manager and then as a partner.

Christian had been in the employment of a firm of shipbrokers in Glasgow and had then spent a few months in his brother's office at Grangemouth before going to Stettin, in Germany, followed by five years in their father's business of timber exporting and small-scale shipowning in his native Norway. So Christian was now, in 1851, well qualified to occupy a responsible position in the latest Salvesen enterprise at Leith and it was in the same year that he married (his wife was also a Norwegian) and settled down in Scotland. They made their home in Charlotte Street (now Queen Charlotte Street) in Leith, a few hundred yards from Christian's place of business, and it was there that five of their seven children were subsequently born.

Two years later, in 1853, the firm was dissolved and George V. Turnbull and Christian Salvesen entered into a new partnership without Theodore and with the slightly altered name of Turnbull, Salvesen & Co. It was later, when he was sole partner, to be called Christian Salvesen & Co and finally, as it is today, Christian Salvesen plc. During the years that followed, but mainly in the 1860s and '70s, the famous Salvesen fleet was built up and, bound for distant seas, sailed out from Leith.

On world markets whale-oil was now a highly valued product and, by the time of Christian's death, his sons were running the largest whaling business in the world. Operations started during the 1890s in the waters around Shetland, Iceland and the Faroes in the north, and did not move south, to the Falkland Islands, South Georgia and the South Shetlands, till 1907. Their first factory vessels were sent out to Antarctica in 1911, by which year they were the world's biggest whaling group, catching 2350 whales during 1910/11 and producing 66,510 barrels of oil. In 1913 they shipped the first consignment of an eventual total of eight hundred penguins from South Georgia for the Edinburgh Zoo.

The First World War was declared the following year,

Christian Salvesen, the Norwegian founder of the world-famous Leith shipping company, who died at his home in Trinity in 1911. (Photograph by courtesy of Christian Salvesen plc.).

but the Salvesen merchant fleet sailed on, not, however, without its share of hardship and, on occasion, of disaster. One of their ships, the *Horatio*, with eleven thousand barrels of oil on board, was destroyed by fire in March 1916, and a year later, when an attempt had been made to start a fire with petrol at Leith Harbour, a serious blaze was only brought under control after the loss of almost all the living quarters, a hospital and a cinema. Another Salvesen ship, the *Coronda*, extinguished the fire but was itself torpedoed by German vessels when outward bound for South Georgia later in 1917. The early post-war period

Charles Waddie, Founder Director of the well-known stationery firm of Waddie & Co. Limited, who lived in Trinity.

had its problems too when serious labour disputes at Leith Harbour were partly responsible for a poor antarctic performance by the Salvesen fleet in 1920 and 1921.

Their merchant vessels braved the German U-boats of the Second World War also when sixteen of their twenty-six ships were lost, including all six floating factories. Whaling operations were resumed after 1945 but the objects of the nautical chase were, not surprisingly, becoming scarce and the last Salvesen whaler returned to Leith in 1963 when the ships were sold after well over sixty years of whaling by the Salvesen family.

In 1870 Christian Salvesen, who received the title of Knight of the Order of St. Olaf in 1891 from the King of Norway, is recorded as being resident at Catherine Bank House, No 172 Newhaven Road (immediately next door to Mr Hunter's Bonnington Academy) but by 1888 he had removed to Mayfield, in East Trinity Road, where he spent the remainder of his life and it was here that his death occurred, at the age of eighty-three, in January 1911. He was buried in Rosebank Cemetery. Mayfield, a gift from the Salvesens, then became a home for sailors' orphans. Dressed in navy blue uniforms, they attended Trinity Academy and went on Sundays to St. Serf's Church on the south-west corner of Clark Road. The home was opened shortly after the end of the First World War and has been succeeded in the house, which has now been considerably enlarged, by the present Cheshire Home.

Edward Theodore, Lord Salvesen, Christian's son who was born in 1857, became an advocate in 1880 and Solicitor General for Scotland in 1905. He died in 1942, having lived in Dean Park House in Queensferry Road which has since been taken over by Daniel Stewarts and Melville College.

During the 1930s Theodore E. Salvesen, JP, was Consul of Norway for Scotland, French Consular Agent and Consul for Finland at the offices of the company at No 29 Bernard Street in Leith. Today the Salvesen organisation is administered from East Fettes Avenue.

After the disposal of the whaling fleet the company eventually diversified into cold storage, quick freezing, transport and even house-building. But it is with their merchant fleet and their world-famous whalers battling their way through the stormy northern seas and the waters of the South Atlantic that the name of Christian Salvesen will always be associated in the Port of Leith.

In the later years of the nineteenth century Gleniffer House in Trinity Road was the home of Mr Charles Waddie of Messrs Waddie & Co, Printers and Stationers at St. Stephen's Works in Stockbridge and still actively in business at St. Stephen's Works in Slateford Road. Along with his elder brother John, he was co-founder of the firm at No 11 Waterloo Place in 1860. In 1867 they removed to No 37 Queen Street and eight years later, still larger premises being required, the factory was established in Stockbridge where ground had been purchased in St. Stephen Street and the new St. Stephen's Works (which were to be extended in 1893 and 1895) had been purpose-built.

In 1873, on the death of a younger brother Alexander, John Waddie left the firm to take over the coal business in Leith which had been run by Alexander and which then became known as John Waddie & Co, Coal Exporters.

Charles Waddie was a well-known advocate of Scottish nationalism and one of the founder members of the Scottish Home Rule Association. At one time he had a conference with Irish home rule leaders with a view to working together for their common aspirations which did not in the event materialise. He died in Gleniffer House in 1912, aged seventy-five, and was buried in Rosebank Cemetery.

At St. Stephen Street Waddie & Co opened a book-binding department (their account books and letter books are still on constant order) and an engraving and lithographic department and even moved into the production of inkstands and quill pens. Further expansion here being impossible, the company removed in 1950 to more spacious premises at No 97 Slateford Road, taking with them the old and by then familiar name of St. Stephen's Works, where they continue to operate at the present time. Still a family business, and still expanding and developing through the use of modern technology, Waddies of Edinburgh celebrated its centenary in 1960 and looks to the future with the same confidence and enthusiasm which have served them so well since the firm laying of their foundations by Charles Waddie and his brother in the nineteenth century.

The coal and coke merchants and colliery lessees, James Waldie & Sons, were known in Leith, Edinburgh and Glasgow till well into the present century, Mr Thomas Waldie living in Birnam Lodge, No 78 Trinity Road, at the end of the nineteenth. With collieries in East Lothian, their chief offices were at No 103 Leith Walk and No 21 Haymarket Terrace, their shipping and country business was conducted at No 46 Constitution Street and they had sub-offices at railway stations and the canal in Edinburgh. The firm had "order offices" as well and these were to be found at Mr Anthony's Cab offices at Goldenacre, at

An advertisement for Gibson's Aeroplanes which were produced in
Manderston Street off Leith Walk, around 1910.

Craighall Road and at Trinity Crescent. The business was
established as long ago as 1784.

It is a long time since aircraft were manufactured in
Leith, but it happened in the early days of flying at the
beginning of the present century. Around 1910 *Gibson's
Aeroplanes* was located at the Caledonian Cycle Works,
No 109 Leith Walk and the planes were built at No 10
Manderston Street where one of the railway arches was
used as a workshop. As could be read in their advertisements, 'Complete Biplanes' were produced at a price range
starting at £450 and with these they were successful
exhibitors at 'Olympia, London, and Brussels Exhibition'.
It was Mr John Gibson, whose home was at 33 Rosslyn
Crescent, who designed and constructed their first biplane
which was then taken to Balerno for engine trials.

The aircraft industry quickly developing beyond the
scope of small, individual companies, this enterprising
concern became John Gibson & Son Ltd, Motor Agents,
Engineers and Coach Builders at Jameson Place and Nos.

107 and 109 Leith Walk, and subsequently at Bonnington Road and Sighthill. This firm was wound up a number of years ago but Gibson Refrigeration, established by George Gibson, a cousin of the founder, was set up at the Leith Walk address and later operated at No 78 Albion Road until its closure in 1988.

The old traditions of enterprise and hard work have their counterpart today in the workshop units and service industries which are now bringing new life to the former scenes of labour and grinding poverty in the Port, and with them have come, as a natural consequence, new houses for the increasing population, new scope for leisure and communal activity, new prosperity, and new and justifiable hope for the foreseeable future.

Further Reading

'Bonnington; Its Lands and Mansions', John Russell in *The Book of the Old Edinburgh Club*, Vol. 19, 1933.

The History of Trinity House of Leith, John Mason, 1957.

Salvesen of Leith, Wray Vamplew, 1975.

The Life and Times of Leith, James Scott Marshall, 1986.

Old Leith at Leisure, James Scott Marshall, 1976.

Old Leith - the Caring Community, James Scott Marshall, 1979.

The Rev. Francis Muir Memorial Volume, Junction Street Church, 1873.

The Provosts of Leith 1833-1920, Edinburgh Room, Edinburgh Central Public Library.

Minutes of Leith Town Council.

The Water of Leith, ed. Stanley Jamieson, 1984.

The Main Drainage of the City of Edinburgh, Edinburgh Corporation, 1955.

Wardie School 1931-1981, Jubilee Booklet.

Frank Worthing - Victorian Recollections of a Family and a House, Joyce M. Wallace, 1975.

Saint Conan's Kirk, Loch Awe, J.C. Martin, 1954 (guidebook)

'Scottish "Athenian" in America', Mary Jane Scott, in *The Journal and Annual Report of The Architectural Heritage Society of Scotland*, No 13, 1986.

Art in Scotland: Its Origin and Progress, Robert Brydall, 1889.

A Concise Dictionary of Scottish Painters, Paul Harris, 1976.

Edinburgh, in *The Buildings of Scotland* series, 1984.

Index